I'm Still Growing

I'm Still Growing

by
Joyce Landorf

THOMAS NELSON PUBLISHERS
NASHVILLE • CAMDEN • NEW YORK

Fourth printing

Published in Nashville, Tennessee, by Thomas Nelson, Inc. and distributed in Canada by Lawson Falle, Ltd., Cambridge, Ontario.

Printed in the United States of America.

Scripture quotations marked TLB are taken from **The Living Bible** (Wheaton, Ill.: Tyndale House Publishers, 1971) and are used by permission.

Scripture quotations marked RSV are from the Revised Standard Version of the Bible, copyrighted 1946, 1952, © 1971, 1973 by the Division of Christian Education of the National Council of the Churches of Christ of the U.S.A. and are used by permission.

Scripture quotations marked "Phillips" are from J. B. Phillips: **The New Testament in Modern English.** Revised Edition. © 1958, 1960, 1972. Used by permission of the Macmillan Company and by William Collins, Sons & Co. Ltd., London and Glasgow.

Library of Congress Cataloging in Publication Data

Landorf, Joyce.
    The high cost of growing.

    1.   Christian life—1960-   I.   Title.
BV4501.2.L31818   1978   248'.4   78-1385
ISBN 0-8407-5129-X

My continued thanks to two gifted gals
Brenda Arnold
and
Sheila Rapp
for their typing, editing, and especially
their spelling!

My special thanks to Pete Gillquist, who by
asking the right questions began this book.

CONTENTS

Chapter One

The High Cost
of Growing

There is an old nursery rhyme that goes,

> Mary, Mary, quite contrary,
> How does your garden grow?

The improbable answer is,

> With silver bells, and cockle shells,
> And pretty maids all in a row.

We smile at the whimsical verse, for we know too well what makes a garden grow, and it has little to do with shells, bells, or statue-like maids lined up in a row.

What farmer, after all, expects his fields to yield a harvest merely by his looking through a seed catalog, choosing his crops, and then settling back in his rocking chair to wait? If he thinks his garden and fields will grow without his cultivating the ground, planting the seed, weeding, fertilizing, watering, and harvesting, he's more off his rocker than on.

Yet in the same improbable, fairy-tale way, I find we often think Christians grow more like Christ every day **without** any action, any suffering, doubts, or pain. It is rather as if we have a little set of doodads here, a bit of mumbo-jumbo there; and a few cockle shells and silver bells later we arrive at full-blown Christianhood. It's as if we become instantly sensitive to both the Holy Spirit and others; then magically we develop into giants of the faith with nothing happening in between. No fuss, no muss, and certainly no hassle.

Not so!

The hard, cold labors of farming are what produce the crops and the rich harvests, and it is just so with our spiritual growth. Growing by pain, stress, doubts, obedience, differences, and past and present situations is what the Christian life is all about. Visible growth is the best thermometer in the world by which to take our spiritual temperatures. It can tell us whether we are alive in Christ or not.

Over twenty years ago I awakened to a new life in Jesus Christ. What I did not know then but know now is that coming to Christ was the event, but **staying** alive in Him is a life-long process.

Not too long after I accepted the Lord I was filled and bubbling over with an enthusiastic desire to tell the whole world about the gospel. I was convinced that since I could sing He would use that talent, and I'd be everywhere singing for His glory.

However, no one asked me to sing and no doors opened, so I questioned the Lord as to how He wanted me to give the gospel to the world.

"Be a wife first, a mother to Rick and Laurie second, and later I'll take care of these other things," came the Lord's quick, matter-of-fact answer. It wasn't **exactly** what I'd had in mind.

I accepted the Lord's "no" and followed His direction, not because I was the marvelously obedient sainted Joyce, but rather because when I examined the alternatives of living outside God's will it scared me to death!

Have you ever pestered, begged, or nagged God with some request, had Him answer no and then days, months, or even years later breathe a sigh of relief at the wisdom of that "no"? I have. In fact, when I think about that first no of the Lord's, I can see Him in my mind's eye, shaking His head, smiling, and I can hear Him saying,

"You see Joyce, I've always known what's best for you. I gave you a "no" answer not because I didn't love you, didn't think you capable or talented enough, or didn't need you to share the good news, but because **you** needed a time to grow."

I know now the Lord wanted me to have twenty years of growing before I wrote a line about it, much less a book! I needed those twenty years. I still need the growing process, and I will have that need to grow until I see Him face to face.

Growing is that intangible moving force that

11

stretches our minds and souls in a thousand directions at once. Yet, why then is there so much misunderstanding, passivity, and just plain fantasizing over growth? And why isn't there an overwhelming desire on our part, as Christians, to grow up?

The reason is simply that growing is something **none** of us considers our favorite love-to-do thing. Generally speaking, it is no thrill to grow. As I recall there was no glamour and no excitement associated in my mind with being wife and mother as there seemed to be in singing for God.

I suppose it has to do with the fact that growing is an action verb. It requires a decision of the will, a commitment to do, or at the very least some kind of change. Most of us loathe moving out of our comfortable ruts and rocking chairs. Yet, growing up in Christ means just that—moving and changing.

Haven't you wondered from time to time why some Christians are so extra special? They add joy to your life even if your eyes only meet in a fleeting glance across a crowded room; or one smile and handshake opens the flow of conversation as if you had been friends for ages. Growing Christians increase your perspective, enlarge your capacity for learning, and leave you filled up beyond measure.

Other Christians drain your supply source, taking so much spiritual energy away from you that when you leave them you are exhausted. Sometimes not even your sense of humor is intact.

As I have observed and talked with hundreds—no, make that thousands—of Christians, the ones who are

12

dynamic and loving people are constantly blossoming, growing, and bearing fruit in Christ. They are not the "arrivers," as Keith Miller would say, but the "becomers."

I have made a list of people whom I believe are **growing** in one way or another. Some of them are not Christians, and so they do not add to my spiritual insight or depth; but they do have a great deal to teach me about growing. My list is entitled "I sometimes wish I were _____ ."

Now, before you think I'm unhappy being me, let me hasten to say, God has made me Joyce Landorf. He has made only one of me, and while on some days I am not too pleased with me, I know I am loved, forgiven—and not only accepted by God, but **chosen.** But the people on my list possess qualities I admire and would like to emulate. As you review the list, I hope you will begin to understand, as I have, the conditions for growth.

I sometimes wish I were. . .

Barbra Streisand. She is a musician's musician who tells her vocal chords to do this and that and this again without losing control, pitch, or beat. And her voice flawlessly obeys.

Martene Craig. She can conduct any group, choir, orchestra, or collection of people set before her without a single qualm. She can also go from the farthest out rock music to the heaviest Bach or Beethoven number without any trace of musical or cultural shock.

Dinah Shore. She comes across on television as an

easy-come, easy-go, relaxed lady. She asks all the right questions and interviews guests with apparently little or no fuss.

Chris Evert. She hits that little white ball over the net with an effortless flick of her wrist.

John Naber. He slices through water with the speed and grace of a dolphin.

Clare Bauer. Beautiful and brainy—inside and out.

Dale Evans. The older she gets, the more she glows.

Corrie ten Boom. Same thing! She glows even though she's had eighty-four years of glowing.

Dick Landorf. He is a banker with everything under control and he never gets lost in the process. He also is the most tough and tender man alive.

Dr. James Dobson. He is a psychology expert.

Dr. Leonard Buchanan. He is an engineering expert.

Dr. Edward B. Cole and **Dr. Keith Korstjens.** They are theology experts.

Dr. James White. He is a surgeon and medical expert.

I could go on, but I'm sure you already have enough to work with. The real point of giving you this list is to show you that the people on it have learned two important truths: (1) what we become is **not** the result of merely possessing a God-given talent, and (2) the high cost of growing must be paid if improvement and eventual excellence are desired.

Saint Peter is quite clear about our talents when he

says, "God has given each of you some special abilities
. . ." (1 Pet. 4:10, TLB).

We all have special gifts, talents, or physical abilities, but the key to real success lies in what we choose to do with them.

For instance,

Barbra was born with that four-octave voice. But developing it, perfecting it, and learning to read music was done in practice rooms and with great expense of time and energy.

Martene has loved music all her life, but it was the hard work and study, not the love, that changed her into the fantastic minister of music she is today.

Dinah, although she comes on television looking relaxed and full of ad-libs, has given serious and careful attention to the biographical material on each guest. In other words she has done her homework and has done it well.

Chris would have stayed on the tennis court in someone's backyard, impressing a handful of family and neighborhood friends, except for the hours of exhausting, determined workouts.

John would have cut a dashing figure at the beach or pool, but he would have never been awarded his Olympic gold medal for his good looks alone.

Clare has never settled for mediocrity in **anything,** so she is always striving for perfection in whatever task is before her.

Dale's newest book, **Trials, Tears and Triumph,** is a study of how God has caused her to grow. For my money she has every right to be an ugly, embittered lady. Yet her incredible losses have been the power behind her glow.

Corrie's glow did not come suddenly. It was not a quick happening, like turning on a light bulb, that ushered her into bright sainthood. No, she grew, expanded, and began her glow in the horrors of the Ravensbruck concentration camp under Hitler's dictatorship.

Dick's tough and tender ways have used up the better part of twenty years. My husband is constantly **becoming** God's man. I can see God's hand on the loom of Dick's life—weaving and working a man of sturdy cloth.

And of course the various doctorates of my friends were not generously bestowed as honorary degrees, but in each case the doctorate was hard earned and obtained at great physical and mental expense.

All of these people, plus many others I have met and talked with, have not been automatically sensational, successful, or obviously super-spiritual. In each case, while there was initial talent, there was an exacting toll paid for growth and development, and there always will be. Maturing and growing, whether it is mentally, physically, or spiritually, is always very difficult.

I suspect many of you agree with that last statement. Even back in high school and college, which of us did not want to cut class, skip school, or play hooky at least once during the semester?

For our own individual reasons we didn't seem to

want to learn any more arithmetic equations, any more spelling words, or any more grammatically correct phrases. And yet growing and learning meant we had to concentrate, study, and work our brains overtime. It would have been a lot easier to duck out of school. And so it is—whether we are talking about the formal academic institutions or the big, real school of life.

So how does a Christian really grow?

1. **Growing is a very slow process that extends over our entire lifetime.**

We live in a world of instant replays. Add water and stir. We are impressed with speed, and so to develop slowly and by God's timing in the midst of our culture is probably one of the most difficult lessons to learn.

We want instant sainthood. We want to immediately find the right words to comfort the bereaving family and friends. We pray for on-the-spot success and spout on-the-spot solutions. We want total recall of the appropriate Scripture verses. And worse than any of these, we glibly quote, "Be patient with me for God isn't through with me yet," but don't mean it for one single second. We are the most impatient people in the world, particularly when it comes to **our own** development. I have talked with many defeated Christians who say, "I just don't understand God's timing in this." What they really mean is "What's taking so long?" and "Why doesn't God hurry up?"

So the first principle of becoming a growing, expanding Christian is to understand that maturing is a

17

slow, never-ending process. It goes on and on. Sometimes growth is like a children's game—we take three giant steps forward and then are made to take one backward. That in itself is enough to confuse and discourage us. Yet growth does not come in a highly regimented fashion. We don't take it three times a day like our morning, noon, and bedtime doses of medicine. It comes in spurts, and usually at a time when we least expect it.

Only God knows how much growing we can assimilate into our systems during one given period of time. So be patient with the Lord and trust His timing. He really is in control, and believe it or not, He knows what He is doing.

In addition to growing covering a long period of time, there is a second factor we must understand about God's process.

2. **Christians often grow and mature best in the heavy, cold darkness of stress, pain, various anxieties, fear, and by all kinds of emotional, physical, and mental suffering.**

The title of Margaret Clarkson's book **Grace Grows Best in Winter** is not only poetic and beautiful, but terribly true.

While it is possible to learn and mature as a Christian during the bright, fair-weather times of our lives, the rate of spiritual development is greatly diminished compared to the rate during the storms of life. Many of us know that when tragedy slams into us with the force of a tornado, or when stress and pain pull all the rugs out from under our feet, the chances of our

18

growing are greatly accelerated and greatly enhanced if we are careful to see them.

I can hear someone saying out there, "Oh, Joyce, God is not a cruel God, inflicting these terrible things on us for our benefit. He does not want us to suffer, to be sick, or to be in pain. In fact, there are many ways to grow in Christ other than through heartaches and stress." Still another person says, "Why, I know for a fact God teaches us to grow through daily devotions, Bible study, discipling groups, and a dedicated prayer life."

To all of this I can say a hearty "Amen!" We do not have a cruel God who gets some weird kick out of seeing us squirm under pressure. And yes, we do grow from good, positive experiences. In fact, I will deal with some of them in a later chapter. But the point is that Christians grow **best** and experience greater results under God-allowed crises and problems.

To some people this concept of God using suffering, stress, and pain to bring forth growth is an intolerable thought. Truly it is one of the most misunderstood and mistaught teachings of our day. Yet it remains firm: the Lord uses all of the hard, cold, difficult things of this world to bring about development and growth. We need to be reminded that He used suffering, adverse situations, and disappointing circumstances in the lives of people mentioned throughout the Bible, and some of them were people who were far more spiritually advanced than any of us. So why do we have such a hard time with the continual problems of suffering?

Basically, we don't want to pay the high cost of

growing, which may mean stress or suffering losses. And secondly, to us these avenues of growth and maturity rarely make sense.

When a young piano student is flailing away at Hanon or Czerny exercises several hours a day, it is very difficult for him to make a great deal of sense out of it. Yet those repetitious trips up and down the keyboard, and the aching muscles that follow, all make a great deal of sense a few years later when he sits down to play a flawlessly executed piano concert.

How easy it is to look admiringly at others, to compare our successes with theirs, or to wish that we could achieve the same level of excellence, and all the while ignore what God wants us to do with our own lives.

There are many other ways to grow and none of them are easy. Growth is expensive, but I encourage you to look not only at the price of growing but also at the rich harvest God has in mind for you to reap.

Chapter Two

Growing Through Suffering

We are never ripe till we have
been made so by suffering.

—Henry Ward Beecher

Pete Gillquist, author and recently turned publishing editor, sat before me. His long, lanky frame covered one end of my couch as he talked.

"Joyce," he said in a quiet probing voice, "you are not just churning out these books one after another like some factory assembly line machine. I've read them, and with each book I find progress and real growth. Something is responsible for the growth in your life."

And then, even more directly and deliberately, he leaned forward and asked, "Tell me, how **do** you grow?"

My reaction was instantly twofold: pleased, yet surprised. I was pleased because suddenly I was a little

21

hazel-eyed, blond-haired girl again. It was as if Pete had taken me over to the measuring marks my mother used to make on the wall, patted my head, and pronounced, "Wow. Look at that! You're two inches taller than the last pencil mark."

Since I have always contended that the Christian life should be a never-ending growing process, it was beautiful to hear my progress being confirmed and to learn that the signs of maturity were showing—at least according to Pete's spiritual yardstick.

But secondly, I was surprised because at no other time during my twenty years as a Christian has anyone ever pointedly asked about my growth in the Lord.

Then a depressing thought surfaced and skipped across my mind. Oh dear, did no one ask because no one could see any evidence of growth? I remembered that marvelous yet disturbing song Dave Boyer sings which in part says, "If you were arrested for being a Christian, would there be enough evidence to convict you?" and for a few moments it gave me quite a bad time. Mentally I moved on.

What an intriguing question—"How do you grow?"

How does anyone grow? Do all Christians mature and develop in specific and identical manners, or do we grow like children—in spurts, with different speeds and intensities? Does God use varied methods and vastly different timetables for us?

Most of all, my conscience pricked me as I sat before Pete because I thought about all the times I have been in the presence of a real, live, growing-before-my-eyes

22

person and failed to ask him or her about their secret ways of growing. It was a depressing thought because I had missed the moment and not taken advantage of the opportunity. I had lost encounters that had been pregnant with learning.

After a few seconds of stunned silence, I came face up to the answer about my own personal growing.

"Pete, if there is evidence of growth in my life—and I fervently pray there is—then it is due to two kinds of suffering."

"Suffering?" Pete tilted his head and looked quizzically at me, and I realized my statement must have sounded vaguely pious, if not downright stilted and stuffy.

I tried to explain.

"Yes, suffering—the **emotional** suffering of my childhood and young adult life long ago, and the more recent **physical** suffering of my life now."

All he said was, "Tell me about it."

Then for the better part of two hours I shared about the two types of suffering that have consistently and inevitably produced and contributed to my spiritual growth.

Recalling the hurts and disappointments that afternoon to Pete was very difficult for me to do and quite painful. Reviving our past in objective honesty usually is.

Much of what I said had to be brought up out of some pretty deep caves within me, and my confrontation with truth was an unsettling yet marvelously healing time. I will never regret or forget the afternoon. But then, growing is always like that—a difficult yet unforgettable experience.

I am firmly convinced that Paul's words, likening us to God's garden, are true, especially when he writes: "In this work, we work with God, and that means that you are a field under God's cultivation . . ." (1 Cor. 3:9, Phillips).

It was Charles Spurgeon, one of history's great ministers of God, who said,

> Oh, to have one's soul as a field under heavenly cultivation, no wilderness but a garden of the Lord, walled around by grace, planted by instruction, visited by love, weeded by heavenly discipline, guarded by divine power. One's soul thus favored is prepared to yield fruit unto the glory of God.

If it is true that we are a garden or a field cultivated by God, I am sure one of the best garden tools the Lord uses in our lives to produce fruit and stimulate growth is the digging trowel of suffering.

How hard it is to let Him dig. Every time He uses suffering to cultivate and aerate the soil around us, we are sure our lives are being uprooted and bound for annihilation.

Yet, quite the opposite is true. God uses his trowels, tractors, and plows with utmost discretion and wisdom, and all that digging produces healthy, growing people.

There are many kinds of human suffering and, of course, the most obvious and "seeable" kind is the physical. For example, the physical pain of a debilitating disease, the chronic pain of a bone or muscle problem, or the wearisome pain of a dysfunction somewhere in our anatomy all produce a wild, ancient kind of suffering.

There is also a suffering that is easily concealed and sometimes hard to identify, but the pain is just as real as the physical suffering. It is the emotional and mental suffering of our inner being. Let's consider further this kind of pain.

Many of us spend a goodly portion of our lives either disguising this pain, ignoring it, or shoving it way down into our subconscious. Some of us manage to forget it altogether, and it lies inside us, locked away out of our view. Nevertheless, this emotional and mental suffering is just as corrosive, wild, and ancient.

Chronologically, the first suffering we generally run into is the emotional suffering of our childhood that often causes the traumas of our early adult years.

I shall not bore you with the specifics and never-ending parade of hurts and disappointments of my own childhood. My early life had its share of positive approval, especially from my mother, but it also had many negative and disappointing factors. I have not revealed those negative factors in past books nor do I intend to start now. And besides, I have a better reason for not sharing the details of my childhood with you. I am wise enough and old enough to know that

25

your painful childhood stories and experiences may very well top mine.

But mark this down somewhere permanently: **Each of us has indeed suffered.** For some it has been to a minor degree. For others the suffering they experienced during childhood has left wounds which are almost irreparable and which, to this day, still fester quietly within them.

Once or twice, here and there, I have met individuals who seemingly have escaped the hassles of traumatic emotional suffering during their childhoods, but it's not too often.

Our own two children are interesting examples. When our twenty-four-year-old son Rick and daughter-in-love Teresa were playing the communications game "Tell It Like It Is," Rick drew a card that read, "Complete the statement, 'One thing I missed during my childhood was. . . .' "

Teresa told me that Rick looked at her and in a "I'm-shocked-you'd-even-ask" tone of voice replied, "Nothing! I missed nothing during my childhood!"

His statement warmed my heart. However, I suspect if we picked and probed long enough and deeply enough, we could come up with a few things Rick might have missed or at least wishes had been different.

However, I am positive our twenty-two-year-old daughter Laurie, who was born with a hearing loss in both ears, would have answered the question in a vastly different way. I need not ask her to know that what she "missed" during her childhood was the taken-for-granted privilege of hearing the soft, quiet sounds of the world around her.

I have often wondered how the specific childhood sufferings of the great giants in the Bible affected their adult lives.

Did David the psalmist ever look back on his lonely life as a shepherd boy and long for it to have been different? Did he ever fantasize about a good relationship with his brothers as opposed to the one he had? Was his later friendship with Jonathan forged out of his family's rejection and lack of approval? I imagine so, and I highly doubt that anyone in David's family fully understood the great poetic, talented genius that tended the family's sheep herds and took lunches to the brothers in battle. Even when young David was anointed king, I doubt that anyone in his immediate family was too overwhelmed by the honor or glory of it.

In any case, we are all products of our childhood experiences. Our adult performance and behavior is programmed like a computer, for better or worse, in our early years.

If it were possible to clearly label people according to their childhood experiences and categorize them into neat little boxes, I think we would need,

• A small box for the low percentage of people who had few or no negative hassles and who have experienced a relatively trouble-free childhood.

• A rather large box for the majority of people who have had a mixture of both positive and negative factors and who have experienced a sometimes insecure and unbalanced, yet fairly routine, childhood.

27

- A medium-sized box for the people who have had more troubling, negative factors than positive and who are still trying to cope with them today.
- A small box for the low percentage of people who never had one single positive influence in their lives and whose childhood produced a torrent of violent and tragic factors from which they may never recover.

When I see those boxes in my head and examine the stories that come out of all of them, I am made aware of a slightly sticky problem, and with reluctance I write about it.

There seems to be a traditional tendency among Christian parents and families to believe that their children, by a magical act of God, will escape all the emotional hurts and bruises of childhood—that they will automatically be in the first box and have a pain-free childhood. It is as if being a church-going, born-again family were a guaranteed security blanket that will protect and insulate each member of the family from any harm.

I can say that statistically the divorce rate, juvenile crime rate, cases of drug abuse, child abuse, incest, homosexuality, and alcoholism (and I could go on) are **definitely lower** in born-again families. Nevertheless, these tragic, horrendous things do happen and are happening in the Christian home of today. Every contemporary Christian counselor, psychologist, and minister has seen the wide path of evidence sin is making in the meadows of Christian lives.

To our sad horror, we have known the Bible teacher who is a child abuse mother; the chairman of the board of deacons who practices incest with his four daughters; the minister of music who leads a double life as a heterosexual and homosexual; the Christian graduate of a Christian college who has turned to drugs and alcohol because her stepfather sexually molested and raped her from the time she was four years old until she ran away from home at sixteen; the once enthusiastic missionary who has returned and is convinced she is absolutely worthless and who now rots in total depression in a back bedroom of her house; or the pastor's wife who has venereal disease because of her husband's affairs. Shocking? Yes, but sadly true.

These people all **exist** within the church. To believe things like this are not happening in the Christian home is an attractive but foolish and highly erroneous philosophy. Scores of ministers, Christian counselors and psychologists, and dedicated laymen and women are unfortunately in the position to verify the fact that just because we claim to be Christians does not mean we are immune to this kind of suffering.

So it comes as a chopping death-like blow to many Christian adults when they have to admit or face either their own or their child's emotional traumas. It is harder still to try to examine the causes or to dig up the ugly roots.

In case your childhood memories are buried too deeply for you to locate immediately, let me give you some examples. These are hurts out of my own childhood and a sampling from those of a great many other Christian adults. All of these conflicts have given their own measure of suffering. I may have missed your particular experiences, but perhaps you can in some way identify.

You may have lived your childhood and young adult life with one, several, or (I pray not) all of these things:

• The death, divorce, or mere absence of one or both parents.

• The complete or partial lack of support, approval, or verbal encouragement from parents or family which has left you with little or no feelings of worth or value.

• The overprotective parent or family member who never let you pay for a mistake, fall on your face, or run out of money—all of which generally did nothing to prepare you for your adult life in the big city.

• The parent or family member who made the home a hellish prison and wrought anguish on each member.

• The spiritual lectures and judgments given hypocritically and without love which were pounded into you by parents, other relatives, Sunday school teachers, ministers, or church members—and which still sting your memory and have left you a spiritual pygmy.

• The confused, frustrated feelings generated by parents who demanded that you honor them as the Ten Commandments prescribed, but then lived fradulent double lives unworthy of that respect.

• The person in your childhood who picked, nagged, harassed, or teased you unmercifully, all under the thin guise of humor but which left your soul badly damaged.

• The continual upheaval and insecure feelings caused by being a transient family, always on the move.

• The inferior feelings you had, in your early teens, because your face or body (or both) was not up to the flawless perfection of a Barbie or Ken doll.

• The continuation of low self-esteem even now as an adult.

• The times of being depressed because you were chronically ill during most of your childhood or you had a crippling or disfiguring major disease.

• The mother or father who would not or could not trust you, and so they continually made false accusations about you and your activities.

• Parents who fought openly or secretly and then tried to force you into taking sides.

• The sting of remembered nicknames of your childhood which has left you sensitive to what you are called still, to this day.

• The mother or father who told you, even reminded you daily, that you were an unplanned child, and so you grew up "knowing" you were an unwanted person.

• Parents whose behavior was rude, embarrassing, or downright hostile and unexplainable.

• Parents who never communicated love or approval to you while you were growing up, but who now talk proudly about you and take the credit for rearing such a successful offspring.

• The struggles of accepting and coping with a mentally retarded brother or sister or the equally frustrat-

31

ing problem of living with a talented person or mental genius in the family.

• The parent or family member who abused you—physically, by punishment turned brutal; sexually, by molestation or rape; or verbally, by an unending stream of devastating criticisms and put-downs.

There are, of course, many more types of emotional suffering, but these experiences, taken from your childhood and mine, are enough for us to examine now.

Bringing those hurts to the surface from the place within you where they now lie and looking at the sufferings of your soul may frighten you to death, but we need healing in these areas. We also need some kind of understanding of our past if we are to ease our frustrations with daily living.

Not long ago, as I was getting dressed in my motel room and preparing to speak at a luncheon, I felt a sharp pain in my chest and discovered an ugly red lump just under my breast.

After my speaking engagement, and later that night, the lump had expanded from the diameter of a penny to the size of a quarter. By the time I returned home two days later, it was hard to ignore because the hard, flaming red core was covering a good portion of my chest.

My doctor uttered his usual "Mmmm" and then said rather matter-of-factly, "It's a large, badly infected sebaceous cyst."

I remember feeling a brief moment of relief, for I had

32

(as all women do) diagnosed it myself as a malignant tumor.

My relief was short-lived, however, because the doctor continued, "I think it's reached a head, so I'll have to cut it open, drain it, and pack it."

The compassionate nurse, one who has stood by our doctor's side for the better part of twenty years, bent close and whispered to me, "It's going to be rough. We can't give you any Novocain for pain as it spreads the infection." I would have flown off that table in a minute had she not outweighed me.

"You mean he's going to open me up here, right now, with nothing but a sharp knife?"

That afternoon I learned the hard reality of it in the worst way: A cyst that becomes infected needs a sharp knife to lance it and clean it out, packing material to let it drain, and new packing material each day until it is healed.

So it is with our storehouse of old, suppressed memories. Sometimes they lie buried in our minds for years, much like my cyst, never giving us too much grief. But then someone says something, or we say something, that triggers an unexpected response from us or them, or we behave in an unexplainable way, and the tiny pangs of hurt begin to be felt. The infection has begun.

Finally, when the circumstances of life become unbearable and reach a "head," it's time for cutting open the box of memories and draining out the odorous pus so that the wound can heal.

If our memories are allowed to fester within us, they can cripple each relationship we try to establish. They can paralyze us daily and, in some cases, permanently. From that same sebaceous cyst, I learned about the length of recovery. I thought that cyst would take forever to heal. But healing comes to us on its own timetable, and so it is with inner emotional healing.

Our inner healing is a little like forgiveness—it must be constantly updated. We do not experience healing in one second flat. It generally plods along like a tired old horse. We must not be impatient with God's inner healings.

Healing also takes many forms and shapes and indeed, like forgiveness, it sometimes has to be run through our computers daily.

These days, these stress-filled days, I have found myself caring a great deal about the memories and the mental health of Christians. I haven't always put such a high priority on a healthy mind. In fact, for a long time after my husband Dick and I became committed believers, I was contented and thrilled beyond belief that God would simply use us in spiritual ways of healing.

Dick's Sunday school teaching in the high school department, his witnessing in his quiet but powerful way at the bank, my singing and speaking—all of these things were being used of the Lord for others' spiritual health, and I truly thought that was enough.

However, that was before I talked with hundreds of Christians who were desperately trying to cope with difficult childhood memories or frustrating present-day situations with in-laws, grown children, and all sorts of other relationships.

My lack of interest in mental and emotional health also came before I took a good look at my own personal inner agonies: certainly long before I allowed myself to look deep within me, and even longer before I let Jesus do His mighty work of inner healing for my childhood infections.

Mental health—yours and mine—is a delicate, slippery, and mysterious subject. God and all of heaven have certainly had their share of my pestering them about it, but because God so truly understands the deep emotional suffering of His children, it is to Him that we must go for help and healing.

Lest you think I have eliminated all emotional hurts from my life and now live a carefree existence, let me hurry to set the record straight. I am still working through many inner conflicting memories, but I don't trudge down those dark tunnels alone. Jesus is ever present. Nor do I set the following guidelines down as the all-American-failproof-ten-easy-step plan, but rather as alternatives or handles that just may ease your troubled mind and help you to cope with life in this distressing world.

1. **With Jesus by your side, go back in time and memory to your childhood.** On a sheet of paper, list some of the hurtful, distasteful events of your childhood and name the people involved. Begin with small hurts and end with the most painful memories. Remember as you write that we all can write a list like this, but most of us will not want to.

I have found that when a person who hurt me in some way when I was a child does or says something now which opens the old wound—even though I am an adult—the pain is worse. I find, too, that generally I cannot immediately find a reason for their actions. However, I noticed a few years ago that when the pain was **intense enough,** I began to be willing to seek the Lord's face on it, and I wrote down my list— unbearable as it was—so that I could begin to sort it out. And it turned out to be my first step toward sanity and a sound mind.

Your list may be short, long, fairly painful, or heavily devastating; but putting it on paper for no one's eyes but yours and the Lord's is as therapeutic to the soul as a hot whirlpool bath is to tired, aching muscles.

2. **Still with Jesus by your side, place your finger on each event and name on the list. As you go down the list, ask the Lord to let you see these situations and relationships from His perspective.** This will not be easy, especially if you have been hurt deeply, but remember—nothing connected with growing ever is! Particularly ask the Lord to show you how limited, handicapped, or crippled those parents, family members, or other persons really were themselves.

We may never know what childhood traumas our parents or brothers or sisters faced when **they** were children. For instance, we may never find out what turned a loving, warm girl into an embittered mother who physically or verbally abuses her children. We may never hear what childhood horror changed a conscientious boy into a dropout husband and father. But chances are very good that they experienced great hurts and humiliations while they were growing up. Our parents and families may never be able to speak of them, but—believe me—emotional and physical suffering has been going on since Adam, Eve, and sin.

Since I have written **Mourning Song,** a book on death and dying, I have been asked to speak at several medical seminars attended by nurses. One of the first things I ask them to do is to mentally take off their pretty, starched caps and lay down their sophisticated scientific knowledge, and crawl into a hospital bed to see the world of medicine from a frightened, sick patient's viewpoint. Very often this exercise marks the awakening of a sense of compassion and empathy. Dozens of nurses have told me that this attempt to see the hospital from the patient's eyes has served as their initial lesson on compassionate patient relations.

We are attempting to gain the same kind of empathy when we ask God to give us His insight and perspective about the people and circumstances in our memories. Besides that, we are told in the New Testament to make allowances for one another's faults. Only love can do it; and sometimes because the hurt is so deep, only God's love channelled **through** us can do it.

3. **With Jesus still beside you, ask Him to show you how to use those haunting, childhood experiences and memories for God's glory, your own good, and for a reconciling relationship with others.**

Once when I was thinking about Bryan Leech's wonderful way with song lyrics, my mind remembered a line from his song "The Hiding Place."

> There is a hiding place,
> a strong protective space
> where God provides the grace
> to persevere. *

I wondered how Bryan knew about the "strong protective space," and how he knew that God would "provide the grace to persevere." When I talked with him recently, I asked him, "Bryan, what type of bending did God do to you in your life to produce such right-on lyrics?"

His answer was not immediate, and during the momentary pause a small voice within me shouted, "Listen up, Joyce, this will be important."

When Bryan did answer, he said simply, "Oh, Joyce, the circumstances of my life are so disappointing."

For the rest of our conversation I felt the sharp edge of God's digging trowel. Bryan shared with me his childhood in England, his troubled parents, his leaving England to come to the strange land of America, his conversion, his loneliness, and his present circumstances, which can only be described as "most disappointing."

By the end of our conversation, it took no ingenious

*Bryan Jeffery Leech, "The Hiding Place" (Tarzana Calif.: Fred Bock Music Company, 1973, 1974). Used by permission.

insight on my part to sense that his remarkable, talented ability with words and music was forged out of the fires of inadequate people, disfigured and warped by their own experiences, and Bryan's circumstances, which would have caused most of us to retreat forever into some dark place, never to peep out. Yet Bryan writes, and he writes eloquently.

Isn't it strange that out of an emotionally impoverished childhood and a life full of setbacks and uneasy alliances, God has been able to turn Bryan's song-writing talents into incredible works of truth and beauty? That's terribly New Testament!

Just today I was reading Paul's account of the marvelous giving record of the Macedonian church. A verse that spoke poignantly about God's "growing methods" was where Paul wrote, "Now, my brothers, we must tell you about the grace that God has given to the Macedonian churches. Somehow, in the **most difficult circumstances,** their overflowing joy and the fact of being down to their last penny themselves, produced a magnificent concern for other people" (2 Cor. 8:1,2, Phillips, emphasis mine).

How beautifully J. B. Phillips translated that when he used the words "difficult circumstances. . . . down to their last penny . . . produced a magnificent concern for other people."

Here again, we see that the very thing that most discourages us can be used of God to develop our talents, our giving abilities, and our concern for others. How like God to give us the grace to see the suffering of the people in our past and present in His

39

perspective, and then to turn those very things into things like Bryan's songs.

Go back and look at David for a moment. Writing the incredible amount of quality poetry found in the Psalms must have demanded David's undivided attention, time, and a lot of hereto unexplored growth-producing suffering. Where did David get his literary ability? Was it not from all those lonely hours out on the hills with only sheep to keep him company?

Did God allow David's childhood to be lonely and hard on purpose? I certainly think so. In fact, I believe God allowed David to be rejected by his brothers in order to bring the boy into complete dependence on his God and to add greatly to his spiritual stature. And while it's true that we need the fellowship of other believers, the number one point of growing is to recognize our utter dependence on God.

It is highly possible that the cold, dark, frightening hillsides of David's youth were where the greatest Psalms were born and where the best of growing took place.

A friend of mine, who knows the painful and intimate details of my past very well, suggested to me that my motivation for writing twelve books in the last nine years was born out of my own "disappointing circumstances" as a child. The same friend also suggested that perhaps I should be extremely grateful for the hurts, rejections, and people-failures in my past, for they have made me the woman I am today.

His point is well taken. For instance, I have often said, "I would never wish or want a mother to lose a

40

child"; but losing my own son David has developed my abilities to be sensitive to the bereavement of any mother, anywhere in the world. Perhaps the childhood traumas and disappointments we have lived through are the very instruments God is using to lift us from being ordinary, routine people to being extraordinarily gifted ones. Perhaps it's those very things that hurt us in the past that now enable us to reach out to others.

Bryan Leech said, "God takes the negative and turns it into a positive." How true, and how like God!

A few weeks ago, I received a letter from a precious woman who is in the process of transcribing my book **Fragrance of Beauty** into Braille. I wondered how she got started in that line of work, and near the end of her letter, she told me she had initially learned Braille to help her young grandson who is blind. I immediately thought "a negative has produced a positive," and then I wondered what the chances would have been of her learning Braille had her grandson been blessed with 20/20 vision.

I wonder, too, if Peter—who had a great deal to say about suffering—might just have been zeroing in on emotional and mental suffering when he wrote, "After you have suffered a little while, Our God, who is full of kindness through Christ, will give you his eternal glory" (1 Pet. 5:10a TLB).

Point No. 1. Our suffering will give us not only pain but glory! "He personally will come and pick you up. . . ."

Point No. 2. God visits those who suffer—per-

haps more than those who do not! "And set you firmly in place. . . ."

Point No. 3. I don't have to worry about getting a place or losing it. "And make you stronger than ever" (1 Pet. 5:10b, TLB).

Point No. 4. Ah, so there is a reason for suffering after all!

The Modern Language translation of 1 Peter 5:10 says God uses suffering to (1) equip, (2) stabilize, (3) strengthen, and (4) forever establish us!

So as you go over your list, know that God is **very** capable of turning our disastrous childhood memories into His own positive, helpful experience. Who knows, maybe your greatest talent lies rooted in your greatest suffering?

4. Now, turn to Jesus, look deeply into His eyes, and ask the hardest thing of all. Ask Him to help you accept His healing, to give you a forgiving spirit toward these people and events so that you can move on. I wonder how often our past keeps us in limbo—neither regressing nor moving forward?

I wonder, too, how much energy is consumed by those of us who are continually trying to grab and reach for that which was unobtainable during our childhoods? Or, I sometimes consider how much time we waste rehashing and analyzing the past—refusing to accept God's forgiveness or healing—only to find we are still being hurt over and over again by the same old hurts.

I guess we optimistically hope our offending parents, family, or relatives will change and treat us differently. But in reality, those who have wounded us in childhood may be continuing to inflict wounds today, and we find the hurts continuing. Or worse, the very person who was responsible for so many conflicts dies, leaving our wounds hemorrhaging and our conflicts unresolved, and we are faced with a thousand grim regrets.

Open your whole heart and being to God's tender, healing touch. He is the only one who knows the extensiveness of your hurt and how to stop the bleeding. As I write this, God is continuing a healing process in me which He began a few years ago. I know first hand that it can be done and that He is able!

I also need to tell you that while I am not totally well, I have left the intensive care ward and am definitely on my way to recovery. That does not mean the situations that have caused my pains have changed. Some people and some negative forces from my childhood remain **exactly** the same today. They have not changed, nor do I expect or hope they will. But **I have changed.** I have begun to accept the Great Physician's work, and healing is happening.

With God's help we can claim Ephesians 4:32: "Instead, be kind to each other, tenderhearted, forgiving one another, just as God has forgiven you because you belong to Christ." (TLB). Especially we can claim the last part about the **way** to forgive and accept others. We can forgive them as God has beautifully forgiven us.

Hannah More wrote these words of wisdom: "A Christian will find it cheaper to pardon than to resent. Forgiveness saves the expense of anger, the cost of

43

hatred, and the waste of spirits." It is this "waste of spirits" or waste of creative abilities that really concerns me when I talk to a person who **will not** forgive family or background.

I hope I am not making this sound too simple and easy, for I know only too well that it is not. But I know God! I know firsthand that God can ease our attitudes into acceptance.

Joseph, whose real-life experiences read like a soap opera and horror story all rolled into one, is a perfect example of what God can do with our past experiences. Special to my heart is the information that after Joseph was made second in command of Egypt, God blessed him with two sons, and I find their names highly significant.

Genesis 41:51,52 records, "Joseph named his oldest son Manasseh (meaning, 'Made to Forget'—what he meant was that God had made up to him for all the anguish of his youth and for the loss of his father's home). The second boy was named Ephraim (meaning 'Fruitful'—'For God has made me fruitful in this land of my slavery,' he said)" (TLB).

We may never get completely over the traumas of the past, but like Joseph we can, with God's gentle leading, begin to heal and move into being the free, real, and loving people God had in mind all along.

Think of it: Even though He knew our parents, our families, and the illogical and disturbing circumstances of our lives, God not only chose us, He accepted us! And then, read this:

Long ago, even before he made the world, God chose us to be his very own, through what Christ would do for us; he decided then to make us holy in his eyes, without a single fault—we who stand before him covered with his love. His unchanging plan has always been to adopt us into his own family by sending Jesus Christ to die for us (Eph. 1:4,5 TLB).

And He did this because He wanted to!

No matter what kind of family life we have endured or enjoyed, God's plan was to adopt us into His family—the perfect family, with no variances, no hurts, and no disappointments!

Reread these verses in Ephesians, and then tune your ear to the voice of God as He whispers down the canyons of your mind, "My child, you are loved, you are wanted, and you belong to Me! My love is breaking the fetters that bind you, so move out. Be real and loving, from this moment on, for you are My own chosen one, and a member of My family!"

Chapter Three

Growing Through Pain

Out of suffering have emerged the strongest
   souls and
The most massive characters are seamed
   with scars—

           —Edwin Hubbell Chapin

Pain and illness mean heartbreak, even if we have strong faith in the Lord. To nonchalantly say, "If you truly know Christ, pain will never get to you" is sheer madness.

Lazarus' illness and death broke the hearts of Martha and Mary, and of Jesus Himself; and He wept with the awful reality of it.

We must be careful when we dismiss pain as being "all in your head," and we must not give glib mini-sermons based on one verse of Scripture that presume to sufficiently deal with the age-old problem of pain. What is very hard to grasp about pain is the simple truth that it is **not** God's will to banish all disease, pain, or death in this **present** age.

I cannot buy the theory that Jesus wants everybody well. If He did, then no real born-again Christian would ever catch a cold or cancer, much less die. This present world is a melee of pain and death, and we must not confuse this world with the sin-free world to come. For now, here on this earth, we have no escape from trials, tragedies, and tears; so how do we cope with the pain of life?

I have been learning much about pain and, while the growing process is rough, it has been quite an eye-opener. I've found that rarely do we like pain or understand its wild ride through our lives. And never have I known one single person who enjoyed pain or looked forward to it.

Yet, here and there, I am meeting men and women of high integrity and maturity. Sometimes their faces are pinched with pain, but their souls beat with a steady, unshakeable joy. They possess that undeniable yet unfathomable peace, and so help me, they glow!

I was pretty sure, at the outset of a painful condition in my jaw four years ago, that the pain would eventually kill all my joy, fade my peace, and certainly erase any glow I might have had. The realization of what pain was doing to me triggered a burning desire to search out how those who glowed with joy and peace in spite of their pain did so.

Let me back up a moment to say that along with the usual (and sometimes unusual) emotional pain of my

past, the progress of my childhood was often hindered
by some kind of physical illness. There were very few
school semesters during which sickness did not
present lengthy interruptions to my education. But
hard physical pain, the kind I now know, did not begin
its nightmarish existence until four years ago.

It seems to me I have been singing all my life. I
started at age three, got very serious at thirteen, and
have sung daily ever since.

Several years ago, during the recording session for
the album "Joyce," I was quite taken back by how
painful those sessions were to my throat. For hours
afterwards, my throat, ears, eyes, and whole head
ached beyond belief. I simply chalked the pain up to
the tremendous stress a recording session always
produces, and tried to let it go at that.

However, in the following months I became aware
of an emerging pattern of pain that followed every
concert or speaking engagement I gave. Again, I kept
telling myself it was just stress, and I felt that if I could
rest, the trouble would clear itself up.

Then four years ago, after speaking for a Family
Forum seminar in Colorado Springs, I awakened in
my motel room out of a sound sleep. It was three
o'clock in the morning and I had a pain that I couldn't
explain away or ignore.

The pain's highest intensity was in my mouth, and I
was experiencing the worst toothache I had ever had.
Not only was it painful, but it was also ridiculously
frustrating because where the pain hurt the worst
there was no tooth.

Nothing I took or did even touched the blinding hurt. It simply blossomed into an "all-teeth" ache, earache, and full-fledged migraine headache; and it pounded its message into me for the rest of the weekend. Exhausted and completely bewildered, I returned home and poured out my story to Dick. Though we didn't know it then, we were about to see just how hot the fiery furnace of pain can really get.

We also did not begin to estimate our growth in Christ, or how this emerging pain would forever change our lives.

When pain enters your life, the first practical and logical step is to pray, and so we did. We prayed for healing and wisdom. I am sure God heard us, but He decided to usher us into His waiting room.

Then, because we got bored with waiting and because God gave physicians brains and medical skills, we sought out some doctors to see if they could find the cause of my pain. It wasn't that we were running ahead of God. We had prayed for healing (nothing happened), but we had also prayed for wisdom; and common sense said we had "to do" something.

After head, ear, nose, and throat specialists ruled out any major problems, it came down to teeth and, finally (as our dentist discovered), my jaw.

Even though the tears were streaming down my face as I sat in the dentist's chair, I was very relieved that something was found to be wrong. I was beginning to suspect that this whole problem of pain was a psychosomatic situation and a figment of my imagination. My sense of humor had vanished, and I wasn't up to appreciating such remarks as "It's all in your head, Honey" because it literally **was** in my head. At least I sure thought so! The pain had become more than an after-concert nuisance—it was coming on daily.

Our family dentist sent me to a specialist, and he confirmed the jaw-joint diagnosis. He found my temporomandibular (jaw) joint in great trauma and began the first of what seemed like endless hours of work inside my mouth.

It seems that during my teen years several back molar teeth were removed, never replaced, and back tooth support was lost. This and other factors have allowed excessive pressure to be put on the jaw. Then, because head, jaw, and shoulder muscles are all inter-related, whenever there is an imbalance, all the muscles are affected and hence the pain.

Now—four years, much excellent dentistry, several thousand dollars, and many prayers and "why" questions later—almost everything that could be done has been done.

The good news: I am not in acute pain every day as I once was. However . . . .

The bad news: Anything from yawning, eating, and laughing to singing and speaking can still set off a twenty-four- to forty-eight-hour pain spree that is simply wild!

You've heard of the woman who talked so much her mouth wore out? Well, I've done it.

I can joke about it now because the pain I'm in today has been very minimal, but let me risk exposure and show you a small glimpse of my thoughts when pain was really controlling me and when my sense of humor was nonexistent.

I was sitting in the Sea-Tac Airport in Washington, in great pain, when I scribbled the following fragmented thoughts on my yellow legal pad of paper.

People are swirling around me, catching planes, collecting luggage, and doing all the nervous things they do in airports.

But it's hard to focus.

Pain is a super-conceited monster who demands, and gets, my undivided attention.

Its huge shape blocks all the people, places, and emotions from my view.

It forces everything out of my mind and commands me to concentrate on its own intensity.

I will not give in to it! But I'm losing my grip.

The sun outside, behind the large expanse of glass windows, has just set and the clouds are gray against a fading pink sky. It's really lovely, and the Seattle-Tacoma waterways are reflecting the delicate pink. Momentarily, I am filled with the gentleness of the evening; but not for long. The beauty does not dull the ever-increasing, throbbing pain.

I haven't even begun my speaking engagement, and I'm already in pain.

Lord, could I go home? If I have to have pain, could I at least be surrounded by loving and familiar people and things?

The dark gray clouds of evening outside have somehow crept inside of me, and now they are clinging to the edges of my soul.

I'm beginning to feel swallowed up by their slimy, wet presence.

Clouds of depression always look and feel this way; thick, wet, and dark.

Is the sun warm and shining anywhere right now?

I don't think so.

Reason begs me to reconsider and alter my "poor me" attitude, but pain wipes logic off my mind's surface, and I'm convinced the whole world is wrapped and wadded up in this cloud of depression.

I can hear those of you who have not experienced prolonged or chronic pain cheerfully advising me to "look on the bright side" or "to remember God's promises" or "to think about something else." Henry G. Bohn once said, "He preaches patience that never knew pain."

At the same time I can see those of you who **have** suffered nodding your head in perfect agreement. My words make sense to you because you've been there. Perhaps your pain has been far more severe, far more debilitating, or has lasted far longer than mine; but we speak the same language, and we are on the same level of understanding.

For those of you who are really hurting right now, I would like to share some insights that have shed light on the problems of pain and have eased my heart on the blackest of pain-filled nights.

The most obvious lesson we all learn from pain is that it truly forces us to trust, and thus to grow. Either we respond to it and blossom, or we run the opposite way, shrivel up, and die. But facing up to our pain is always brutally hard, for the most obvious dilemma of pain is the ancient question **Why?**

Is having pain in our lives really allowed by God? Could God, in all good conscience, do such a shockable thing? And what's more, does God ever really use pain in a positive way?

Early in my pain, four years ago—or sitting in Sea-Tac Airport that day—I would have shouted, **"Absolutely not! God does not allow us to be destroyed by pain!"**

But because of some courageous suffering people, some startling few books, and some lovely but firm times of God's guiding hand, I now make the following statement:

I hate pain and suffering in any shape or form. I despise the finger of pain that has painted purple shadows beneath my eyes. I cringe when pain carves lines into my face with its sharp knife. I weep when pain capriciously flys away for a short spell, leaving me exhausted, drained, and of very little use to anyone.

But . . . .

Pain has caused me to grow. I have earned my master's degree in "coping" from the high-priced school of pain, and I have seen my husband and children become giants in the faith.

I refuse to run from pain any longer. I still do not like it, but God has definitely brought pain into my life; and while I personally think it is the most difficult of all ways to grow, it certainly is very sure.

Here are some of the most tangible lessons God has

taught me through my experiences with pain. They may not be the exact lessons you have learned, and they may not ease your heart completely. Your pain and questioning heart may only be answered in God's own original way, but I hope these words of mine pour some soothing ointment directly to the hurting part of you.

The Communion of Pain

The loneliness of pain has caused me to call my daughter or daughter-in-love and say, "I'm in such terrible pain today, I can't do anything here. How about going window shopping with me?" And often I have been able to crash through pain's lonely barrier for a few hours at least.

So, when in pain we turn to others to find communion. During the past four years I have read everything having anything to do with pain, and I have talked with hundreds of people about pain—either their own or a loved one's. When I wasn't in extreme pain, I looked carefully at the whys of pain, the healing of it, and the continuance of it.

Each time Dick and I prayed for the Lord to heal my jaw, and we **do** believe in divine healing, the Lord's answer was the same—not now. Even this afternoon I asked again and heard the same familiar response.

This has been the most difficult answer God has ever handed down to me, yet either I believe He knows what He is doing and that He is in complete control of

55

my life, or I don't. Either I am willing to accept this pain as His will, or I am not.

I have always felt that if I could gain some insights on pain, the acceptance would be a little easier. So I began a search for not just the "why" of pain but for the "how" of coping with continuous or chronic pain.

I'm not sure if I can adequately share all my findings regarding pain because aside from the physical beating it brings, it is also a highly emotional issue.

Pain to me is a very real person, and I can see his face quite clearly in my mind's eye. Quite simply, I hate him, and that should give you an idea of how emotional I am over this.

If you, dear reader, have ever suffered even a fair amount of physical pain, you know too well that people (even pastors, doctors, and counselors) who have experienced very little pain firsthand and thereby are calloused to the work of pain, seem to come out of the woodwork to surround and advise you. The man called Pain is nowhere near as real to them as he is to those who have languished under his whippings. Yet these cheerful, unpained souls become veritable towers of advice and expertise.

They tend—

> to find instant solutions,
>
> to claim instant healings,
>
> to find instant examples of our poor diet or lack of proper vitamin intake,
>
> to know in an instant what spiritual blockage is holding up our progress,

to freely share their instant spiritual and medical
diagnosis.

But, worst of all, they tend
to instantly reacquaint us with the stench of
phony advice, and there is no communion between us.

Your church and mine has its percentage of people
whose pain-free existences have taught them that no
pain is too great or too overwhelming for them to
handle with a little help from God. While I understand
their well-meaning and sincere attitude, I am convinced they are sincerely wrong: and this is why I am
speaking out so strongly.

**People in pain do not need one more painful
thing in their lives.**

Gordon McAllister, a young man who has survived
five brain surgeries and now lives with yet another
tumor quietly resting against his brain, said, "Some
Christians actually torture those in pain by the
thoughtless things they say."

Over the past years I've received my share of unso-
licited and less-than-helpful advice. Much has come
by mail, some by phone, some in personal encounters,
and a few disheartening times by sermons in church.

But little or no communion came with those con-
tacts, and the feeling that I would forever endure this
pain alone began to strangle me. About the time I
thought I had been abandoned and was frustrated the
most about my pain, it occurred to me that perhaps I
should change the specifics of my prayers. Instead of

bombarding heaven with requests—no, **demands** is a more accurate term—for my immediate healing, I decided to stop asking and begin listening.

Once more I heard the still, small voice say, "Not now," and so I quit badgering the Lord about healing. I admit to mentioning it every now and then, however, because I love the verse, "Ye have not because ye ask not." However, mostly I'm quiet about my personal healing.

I began to pray about my encounters with people. I told Him I was lonely and dreamed of having communion with Him and some earthly being who would understand. I asked God to place in my path people who had grown because of pain. I dearly longed to hear their godly, experiential advice. I also asked Him to lead me to books and sermons that would heal the inner questions and hurts.

Slowly it began to dawn on me that there were people around who, unlike the physically well "advice givers" had suffered with cataclysmic pain. These were people who would have something very valid and very healing to say to me, and so I prayed in earnest and began to search them out.

The Lord answered those prayers and He moved— slowly at first—to turn my face, heart, and mind in their direction. It was as if the Lord Himself slipped a few drops of His own quiet confidence into my coffee cup one morning, and while the pain was not erased, I felt that out in the big bad world somewhere was a person, a book, a letter, or a sermon that would teach

58

me about living with this monster named Pain. It was my first measure of hope.

As I have learned to pray not for healing but for opportunities to learn, my insights and sensitivities have really been sharpened to a razor's fine edge. For instance, whenever I pick up a book dealing with pain or talk even briefly with someone about the problems of pain, I can tell almost instantly if the writer or speaker has gone to the school of pain or is merely an over-the-wall observer. We either take communion together or we don't.

The people acquainted with suffering have this in common: they **rarely** give quick, pat answers. And when they speak, I am aware of the expense and the high cost of their marvelous wisdom.

Those who suffer also have something else in common: they always touch and soothe the spot deep inside me that hurts the most. They have the genuine gift of comforting others.

Years ago, just before we lost our infant son David, our friend Al Sanders introduced me to the books of Martha Snell Nicholson. What a marvelous comfort her words have been! But no one, not even our gifted and sensitive friend Al, could have guessed the communion between her words and my pain, or what those books would bring to me these past months.

Mrs. Nicholson had five major diseases. She was confined to her bed, unable to move anything but her feet and hands, and in constant pain. Yet in a book no longer in print, she said, "Every morning I awake with quick wonder in my heart and wonder what bright new gift He will give me today."

Her struggle with pain taught her many lessons, but her poem "When He Putteth Forth His Own Sheep, He Goeth Before Them" records how she coped with the loneliness pain produces. The words take on special meaning when you realize the poem was written after her doctor wrote on his report, "Case too far advanced to respond to treatment."

I could not walk this darkening path of pain alone.
The years have taken toll of me;
Sometimes my banners droop, my arms have grown too
    tired,
And laughter comes less easily.

And often these my shrinking cowardly eyes refuse
To face the thing that is ahead of me,
The certainty of growing pain and helplessness . . .
But O, my Lord is good, for He

Comes quickly to me as I lie there in the dust
Of my defeat and shame and fear.
He stoops and raises me, and sets me on my feet,
And softly whispers in my ear

That He will never leave me—nay, that He will go
Before me all the way. And so,
My hand in His, along this brightening path of pain,
My Lord and I together go!"*

Dr. Ralph Byron, a surgeon at City of Hope Hospi-

*Martha Snell Nicholson, **Heart Held High** (Chicago, Ill.: Moody Press, 1954). Used by permission.

tal, once said that the greatest fear a cancer patient experiences is that at some point in time he will be abandoned. Mrs. Nicholson's poem pushes through that great fear by giving us hope in the words "My Lord and I together go!"

Her response to pain is in the following poem. We who have suffered know all too well about the kind of exhaustion described here.

IN A HOSPITAL

Too tired to think, Lord,
Too tired to pray.
Words come so hard, Lord,
What could I say?

Too tired to feel, Lord,
Aught but this pain.
Through what long nights, Lord,
Here I have lain!

Sometime I'll work, Lord,
Sometime I'll pray,
Praise and adore Thee,
But not today.

Blessed assurance,
He understands.
Just let me rest, Lord,
Safe in Thy hands.*

*Martha Snell Nicholson, **Heart Held High** (Chicago, Ill.: Moody Press, 1954). Used by permission.

Relating to honest words like these comes very easily. If you have experienced prolonged pain, you will remember how difficult it is to pray. How I loved Mrs. Nicholson's refreshing words. She didn't pick up a heavy bag of guilt for being too tired to pray; she simply accepted it as the way of pain. Then she trusted God's understanding heart and rested in His love. How beautiful!

Mrs. Nicholson also knew exactly how we would despise pain, but she longed for us to prepare ourselves for its eventuality and existence.

Her analogy of pain being a river into which a child dips his feet is a masterpiece of teaching. She called it,

FIRST SUFFERING

Pain is a river, and today
My very little Sweet,
Into its dark and turgid depths
You dipped your small white feet.

It was the first time you had felt
The touch of grief or woe;
You shrank from it and wept; and yet,
Dear heart, you had to know

Though pain is part of life, our God
Makes bitter waters sweet—
You took a step toward heaven when
In pain you dipped your feet. *

*Martha Snell Nicholson, **Heart Held High** (Chicago, Ill.: Moody Press, 1954). Used by permission.

From the communion of her writings, I have seen so clearly that healing very well may not be God's will. Only my will would claim healing; but so often God's will chooses to use pain, **not** healing, to do His work.

Would Mrs. Nicholson's poems have soothed my heart and drunk communion with me today if they had not been written out of pain? I doubt it. Yet, I'm sure she longed for instant healing. I rejoice that she accepted her suffering, wrote in all honesty about it, and was willing to share what the Lord was teaching her.

Though Mrs. Nicholson has been with the Lord for some twenty years now, her words still find communion with my soul, and over and over again I am drawn back to her choice books of poetic love.

Since I have prayed for encounters with people and books, the Lord has not only reminded me of past helps, like Mrs. Nicholson's work, but He has dropped into my lap very present-day people and writings.

I remember one night not long ago when I had given up eating dinner because the pain in my jaw was so acute. I was unable to disguise the level of pain, and so my face registered the full force of it. Dick eventually lost his appetite, and we dragged ourselves through the evening. By 9:00 P.M. we simply sat on the couch together—not talking, watching TV, or reading, but just sitting there—when our doorbell rang. Dick answered it, but I didn't have the strength nor the hospitality to get up. In fact I didn't even look up until both Mary and Keith Korstjens were in the room before me. (Mary is my "millionaire" friend who is paralyzed with polio and about whom I wrote in **The Richest Lady in Town.** Her husband, Keith, is our dear friend too and one of our pastors.)

Keith pushed Mary's wheelchair to Dick's side, and then he dropped to his knees in front of me. He took my hands in his, put his head on my lap, and wept.

No one called them, no one set up the appointment, no one told them I was in deep pain; but as they were driving home earlier that evening, they both knew they should stop by the Landorfs'.

After Keith slowed down his tears, he simply poured his heart out to the Lord. He voiced all the "why" questions I had screamed within my heart. He spoke honestly of his inability to make any sense out of all of this, and, in a very gentle way, he reminded God of His promises in the Word.

My pain did not go away or even ease, but the four of us and Jesus Himself took communion together that night, and I shall never ever be the same again.

As my family and friends have been drawn into this involvement with pain, the cords of love have grown between us and have strangely bound our hearts together. Our daughter Laurie has not only prayed with and for me, but has merely sat and cried with me. No money can buy that kind of gift.

My daughter-in-love Teresa once told me that whenever I was in severe pain on Rick's day off, he would stop whatever he was doing once an hour and pray for me. I'm sure my pain has given rise to some in-depth power in his prayer life. Even today, Teresa's dear voice said over the phone, "We'll be praying."

I have felt the presence and power of my sister's and father's prayers in spite of the fact that both live far from me.

But the communion pain has wrought between Dick and me has been the sweetest. Over and over I have lain back my aching head while he repeatedly applied the steaming hot towels to my face, and I've cried with love as he whispered, "Oh, Joyce, if only I could have this pain for you."

While it's true that pain can come slamming down like a wedge of steel between two people in a marriage, it is also true that God can use pain as His own special velvet cords of love to bind a marriage firmly together.

Every once in awhile I have to remind myself that were it not for this hideous pain, I would know nothing of this kind of communion with Jesus and others.

The Compassion of Pain

Over the last four years I've become aware of a curious phenomenon happening in my speaking engagements and during my personal conversations with people.

I can be speaking to an audience of five hundred people or of just a few, but very quietly and clearly I can spot and zero in on the person who is hurting the most.

"Whom have you lost?" I asked the lady in front of me.

"My father and sister," she answered, and then added, "How did you know?"

I told her I didn't know about her father or sister, but I saw pain and loss written across her face.

Before me, from my file on pain, is a letter from that same woman. Her note to me begins with the words, "I am the lady with the 'look of pain' you saw and spoke to on Friday the 19th of September at the Christian Writers' Conference held at the Marriott Hotel."

In my mind's eye I can see her face yet. Her letter confirms some very real and frightening fears she was experiencing and she ends by thanking me for being such a sensitive person.

Would I be so alert to the hidden hurts and submerged suffering of others if I had not felt the icy fingers of pain in my own soul? I doubt it. And this kind of an encounter is happening to me over and over again.

I now realize that my mother was able to do the same kind of thing in the years before she died. She always made a beeline for someone in a room full of people, and nine times out of ten it was a person who was desperately troubled, hurting, and needing her. I used to think her instant rapport with hurting people was because God had given her the gift of discernment. Maybe He gave her that too, but now I'm more inclined to think it was her own ever-growing battle with the pain of breast cancer and her willingness to let God use it. Her pain led her into instant compassion for others.

It seems to me that once we have experienced any type of bout with pain, especially prolonged pain, we will have no trouble recognizing it in someone else's eyes. But this is only true if we ask God to use our pain to His glory.

We all have known people who have experienced great pain but have never asked the Lord to use it and so they have become bitter; they are forever whining or complaining. They not only offer no compassion to those in pain, but they are very difficult to be around.

David the psalmist said, "It is good for me that I have been afflicted; that I might learn thy statutes" (Ps. 119:71, KJV). It seems he needed a reason for his pain, just as we do; and **without** complaining, he asked for lessons from the Lord.

David learned those lessons well, for when we are really suffering, how often do we turn to the Psalms? Almost always because David had been deeply hurt and God was able to translate his pain into compassion for others.

Long after David wrote the Psalms, Paul wrote to the Thessalonians, "For he [God] is using your sufferings to make you ready for his kingdom . . ." (2 Thess. 1:5, TLB).

As I mentioned earlier, I have read everything I can find on suffering, pain, and healing. The other day I picked up a small book that dealt with the "whys" of pain.

The author did an incredible thing. He reduced the problems of pain to four simple points:
1. There is no reason for pain and so I should not look for one.
2. I should accept pain. Period.

3. I should memorize and claim Romans 8:28.

4. Then, I would "know" that all pain is ultimately for my good.

The author's conclusions taught me one thing—he has never in all of his life suffered much more than an infected hangnail! Or if by some chance he has suffered, I know he never asked God to teach him how to really use it.

I was not comforted, enlightened, or helped by that book—only disgusted. Later, I had to ask the Lord's forgiveness for my rotten attitude because the man, through no fault of his own, wrote out of good intentions. However, we who have suffered could not have communion with that author; and he, because he knew no reason for suffering, could offer no words of compassion.

About the same time I flung his book down in despair, my friend Sally sent me Rev. Charles Swindoll's newest book, **For Those Who Hurt.** Since Chuck Swindoll is no stranger to me and had already been used of God in my life regarding pain, I eagerly read his book. The unbelievable difference between Chuck's book and the other one was almost humorous.

Both books dealt with the whys of pain; both were beautifully and rightly based on Scripture; both were about the same number of pages in length; but, while one book said almost nothing, Chuck Swindoll's book said **everything.**

I phoned him.

"Do you know what I really like about your book, Chuck?" I was almost shouting. "There is not one

single cliché in the whole thing! How and what produced such a marvelous, truthful book?" I asked.

Then, for the better part of an hour, Chuck gave me a
rather quick but intense biographical sketch of his
childhood traumas, his emotional pain during adoles-
cence, the physical pain of family members, and in
general, the hurts of his own heart.

No wonder his rare book reaches out and embraces
me with compassion. We have walked the same roads,
fallen in the same valleys, and reached the same as-
tonishing conclusions: one of the ministries of pain is
to give us the ability to comfort others in **their** pain.

How else can God do what He promised? He said
He would be our comfort, but how is this realistically
possible unless God comforts **through** us?

This is exactly how the book **For Those Who Hurt**
was born.

The book was first preached and then written because a couple of years ago Chuck looked over his
pulpit and accurately read the facial expressions of one
of the men seated in the congregation. The man
seemed to be disintegrating with his hurt because his
daughter had just run away from home for the
seventeenth time.

"When I saw how deeply this father was hurting,"
Chuck told me, "I asked God to give me a message that
would heal his hurt and answer the need of his brokenness. After dinner that night I wrote the sermon
and later the book about 2 Corinthians 1:3–11."

I am predicting that Rev. Charles Swindoll's rele-
vant little book, borne out of the compassion of a

sufferer, will be mightily used of God. That's an easy prediction because it takes one in pain to know one. Often when we ask God to really use us, He draws on the most painful experience of our lives and turns it into honest compassion.

Read again that familiar passage by Paul, 2 Corinthians 1:3–11:

What a wonderful God we have—he is the Father of our Lord Jesus Christ, the source of every mercy, and the one who so wonderfully comforts and strengthens us in our hardships and trials. And why does he do this? So that when others are troubled, needing our sympathy and encouragement, we can pass on to them this same help and comfort God has given us. You can be sure that the more we undergo sufferings for Christ, the more he will shower us with his comfort and encouragement. We are in deep trouble for bringing you God's comfort and salvation. But in our trouble God has comforted us—and this, too, to help you: to show you from our personal experience how God will tenderly comfort you when you undergo these same sufferings. He will give you the strength to endure.

I think you ought to know, dear brothers, about the hard time we went through in Asia. We were really crushed and overwhelmed, and feared we would never live through it. We felt we were doomed to die and saw how powerless we were to help ourselves; but that was good, for then we put everything into the hands of God, who alone could save us, for he can even raise the dead. And he did help us, and saved us from a terrible death; yes, and we expect him to do it again and again. But you must help us too, by praying for us. For much thanks and

70

praise will go to God from you who see his wonderful answers to your prayers for our safety! (TLB).

We suffer pain and hurt as God allows it, but we never suffer needlessly. No! Our suffering prepares us as nothing else can to identify and recognize pain in others and to comfort with wisdom and tenderness.

About the time I was wondering how my pain would ever produce compassion in me, I received this letter from Dr. Keith Korstjens, my friend who has wept and prayed for me over the years. His letter said, in part,

> These past weeks I have asked the Lord so many times to give some explanation for the awful pain you have been enduring.
>
> It's so human to want to know the "whys" of His workings. At any rate, what He has told me so far is probably not new to you at all. You have known, or at least expected, this for some time now. It's nothing spectacular, yet it helps me put your present hardship into some kind of focus. It's just this:
>
> Your books have each come out of great personal and deep experience. Sometime in the future you will write to help the one who endures great **physical** pain.
>
> **His Stubborn Love** speaks to heartbreak; **Mourning Song** helps the one with turbulent feelings about death; **The Richest Lady in Town** addresses itself to a hundred or more common inappropriate attitudes that plague our daily lives.
>
> Someday a book by you will speak to the thousands who suffer physical pain but do not understand why.

I pray, dear Keith, this is the book.

The Sharing of Pain

The concept of "sharing pain" is difficult to grasp, yet Scripture confronts us with this idea over and over again.

Remember earlier when I wrote about emotional pain? I said that as believers we are part of God's family. Read what Paul said we should expect because of our family ties:

> And so we should not be like cringing, fearful slaves, but we should behave like God's very own children, adopted into the bosom of his family, and calling to him, "Father, Father." For his Holy Spirit speaks to us deep in our hearts, and tells us that we really are God's children. And since we are his children, we will share his treasures—for all God gives to his Son Jesus is now ours too. But if we are to share his glory, we must also share his suffering (Rom. 8:15–17, TLB).

In 2 Corinthians 1:7, Paul referred to those who are "partakers of the sufferings." And to the Christians at Philippi, Paul wrote, "For to you has been given the privilege not only of trusting him but also **suffering** for him" (Phil. 1:29, TLB, emphasis mine).

In that same letter he wrote, "That I may know him, and the power of his resurrection, and the **fellowship** of his sufferings, . . ." (Phil. 3:10, KJV, emphasis mine).

In a letter to Timothy, Paul said,

> I am comforted by this truth, that when we suffer and die for Christ it only means that we will begin living with him

in heaven. And if we think that our present service for him is hard, just remember that some day we are going to sit with him and rule with him. But if we give up when we suffer, and turn against Christ, then he must turn against us. Even when we are too weak to have any faith left, he remains faithful to us, for he cannot disown us who are part of himself, and he will always carry out his promises to us (2 Tim. 2:11–13, TLB).

Evidently, Paul was saying that if we refuse to share the Lord's suffering, we will be faced with joyless consequences.

Peter's words do the most to convince me that sharing in the Lord's suffering is part of the Christian's upbringing. I can hear Peter's deep and resonant voice, mellowed through time by the Holy Spirit, saying, "This suffering is all part of the work God has given you. Christ, who suffered for you, is your example. Follow in his steps" (1 Pet. 2:21, TLB).

Probably his most precious words of encouragement are found in this passage:

Dear friends, don't be bewildered or surprised when you go through the fiery trials ahead, for this is no strange, unusual thing that is going to happen to you.

Instead, be really glad—because these trials will make you partners with Christ in his suffering, and afterwards you will have the wonderful joy of sharing his glory in that coming day when it will be displayed. (1 Pet. 4:12,13, TLB).

In other words, my attitude toward pain should be

73

one of gladness because pain is the very thing that makes me "partners with Christ."

My friend Gordon, with brain surgeries behind him and a dormant tumor lying in his brain now, said wistfully to me, "I miss not being seriously ill." Since I had never heard anyone say such a thing, I questioned him about his statement.

He explained, "It's just that when I was about to have surgery, or when my tumors were growing incredibly fast and my very existence was in jeopardy, I was closer to the Lord than anytime I've ever known. I miss that."

The words of my friend Gordon and all these Scriptures have convinced me that although I can believe in the Great Physician's power to heal our pain-saturated lives, I must also realize that suffering is a lesson in sharing. That lesson is designed to teach us to eventually share in God's holy glory.

I have just finished writing a biblical novel on Martha. While doing my research, I was made especially aware of the nature of Jewish hopes and dreams.

The Jews desperately wanted and certainly felt they needed a **reigning** Messiah, but that is not what they got. Jesus came as a **suffering** Messiah and many Jews never understood that concept.

Neither do we, really. After all, we want Jesus to come into our lives like a great sovereign king and set everything in order. We expect Him to banish all pain and suffering from the kingdom. So when He comes and does **not** put an end to our pain but leads us **into** and **through** suffering, pain, and disappointments, we are as frustrated and confused as the Jewish patriarchs of long ago.

We halfheartedly say, "I guess the Lord knows why, but I sure don't!" We have no concept of suffering **with** Jesus. Nor are we willing to see that we will never have a totally reigning Messiah in our earthly lifetime. We will fully know Jesus as sovereign King and Messiah only in heaven.

If I take time to reread the Bible's words on suffering, somehow the burden of pain is easier to bear, especially when I remember that Jesus and I share it together.

Charles Haddon Spurgeon once wrote, "As sure as God puts His children into the furnace of affliction, He will be with them in it!"

The Blessing of Pain

Could there be such a thing as a blessing in and during pain? Yes, and here are just three ways we experience those blessings:

(1) pain is temporary;

(2) pain can be creative; and

(3) Jesus really does provide the strength to endure.

One dear woman wrote to me after the death of her thirty-eight-year-old son and said in part, "We saw some **immediate** healings during his lifetime, but then we saw the **ultimate** healing of his death and homegoing."

I find no conflict here. In many cases God does heal here and now—sometimes **immediately**—and our hearts long for this to happen; but other times, He uses the "ultimate" healing of a heaven-going experience. Still, pain is temporary if we look at it in the light of time and all eternity.

Just yesterday I talked with Linda whose little two-year-old daughter has a severely damaged brain. Although Amy is unable to do anything a healthy two-year-old can do, her mother said, "Oh, but Joyce, Amy's problems are temporary! So temporary! Someday—maybe only after we reach heaven, but someday—Amy will be whole and well."

A hundred years ago a man, whose name has been forgotten, wrote of pain and said, "Pain is lent to us for just a little while that we may use it for eternal purposes. Then it will be taken away and everlasting joy will be our Father's gift to us, and the Lord will wipe all tears from off our faces."

Last year, when I was afraid this pain in my jaw was not temporary but permanent, the same friend who gave me Chuck Swindoll's book sent me one of his taped sermons.

I listened to Chuck's exposition of Romans 8: 17–27 while I was driving on the freeway, and several times I nearly caused a pile-up. It's hard to cry and drive at the same time. But it was the first time I had put the concept of sharing Christ's suffering into the same box with my pain. It was this tape that caused me to search the Scriptures and formulate my opinions on sharing Christ's suffering.

Chuck also brought Romans 8:17–27 into a most meaningful focus in another way. He did not talk of Romans 8:28, that beautiful diamond of a verse, and I'm glad he didn't. I wasn't ready for it at that time. What he did say loudly and clearly was that I would have suffering, but it would be nothing compared to the glory God would give later.

In other words, my pain was temporary. What a truth to learn while experiencing a jaw ache!

I wrote a letter thanking Chuck for the message of his tape. I did not ask for or expect an answer from him, yet his reply was definitely of the Lord. He wrote,

Dear Joyce:

I'm touched.

Really.

Your moving, heartrending response grabbed my inner man like a vice. Little did I know my words would ever get back to you and be used to strengthen you.

It's about time! You've invested years in giving, my friend. I'm pleased God allowed you to **receive** some specially wrapped, carefully chosen words.

What is it Solomon calls them? Apples of gold in pictures of silver? He framed them just for . . . just for **you.**

Of course, your groaning and pain concern a host of us who love you, Joyce. Rest assured that none of us know why it hasn't been relieved.

And so . . . we wait with you.

Touched.

Really.

Your friend,

Charles R. Swindoll

His words, "And so . . . we wait with you," have tiptoed across my mind in the middle of one pain-filled day after another. Following always behind Chuck's words is the still, small voice of the Holy Spirit saying, "It won't be too much longer; this is only temporary, Joyce."

When I ask the Lord to heal these painful jaw joints and I hear His now familiar, "Not now," I can truly say it's easier to wait—knowing the blessing of pain is that it is temporary and that God gives me strength to endure.

Martha Snell Nicholson once wrote,

We are now His broken things. But remember how He used broken things, the broken pitchers of Gideon's little army, the broken roof through which the palsied man was lowered to be healed, and the broken alabaster box which shed its fragrance over the broken body of our Savior. Let us ask Him to take our broken hearts and to **press upon them further suffering** to give us a poignant realization of the suffering of all the world. Let us ask Him to show us the endless, hopeless river of lost souls. This will break our hearts anew; but when it happens, God can use us at last.*

"Now we are His broken things," she wrote, which implies that someday we will be made whole. This brokenness, used for God's purpose, is only temporary.

*Martha Snell Nicholson, **Heart Held High** (Chicago, Ill: Moody Press, 1954).

78

One other blessing of pain is its ability to force us to be creative. The first time I realized pain could be used in a creative way was when I read **The Mystery of Pain.** It was written by a pastor, Paul J. Lindell, who was dying of cancer. His book opened up a whole new door to my thinking on pain.

He wrote, "Pain can help to illuminate our calling!" When I read that sentence the first time it didn't make too much sense. Then I began to count some of the creative things that pain has really produced.

The emotional pain of a mongoloid child's life and death has produced Dale Evans' book **Angel Unaware.** The pain of five diseases forced Martha Snell Nicholson to write prose and poetry unparalleled in present-day writings. Studies have shown that the pain of childhood or present-day illness has, over and over again, produced miraculous and beautiful things in the lives of many highly successful people.

The best example of pain and suffering illuminating a calling is found in Jesus and the suffering He experienced on the cross.

The writer of Hebrews wrote, "Jesus . . . who for the joy that was set before him **endured** the cross . . ." (Heb. 12:2, KJV, emphasis mine).

Our Lord understood full well that the cross was one of the stipulations of His work on earth and part of His joy was a product of His pain. But He **endured,** and forgiveness for you and me was creatively brought into existence. What a Savior!

Just this past week, Lois Chilton, a returned missionary from the Philippines, told me of a girl named Martina.

Martina was young, beautiful, and very bright. She left the missionary compound in Manila to go up north and teach Bible classes in English and three other dialects.

Not too long after Martina was gone, she wrote Lois and said she was experiencing a "funny numbness in her feet" and was coming down to Manila for some medical help. The doctors in Manila diagnosed her problem as the worst type of leprosy and gave her a very short life expectancy.

Lois said, "When we visited her at the leprosarium the next few months, we could hardly bear to see her." Martina's beautiful face had crumbled and disintegrated very quickly. But God did an amazing thing. For even though Martina was dying, she organized and taught four Bible classes. God blessed her work so much that she was able to start a small church there on the grounds of the leprosarium. That church still goes on today.

Before Martina died and in one of her last letters to Lois, she wrote of all the exciting opportunities she had participated in and ended her letter with the words, "I praise God for the gift of leprosy!"

Pastor Lindell's words about pain could certainly be said of Martina. God sweetly taught her about the blessings of pain and in the process gave her a ministry which will go on past the borders of our time and will march right into eternity.

But how did Martina endure? How do any of us endure?

Paul told the Corinthians, ". . . God will tenderly comfort you when you undergo these same sufferings. He will give you the strength to endure" (2 Cor. 1:7, TLB).

The prophet Isaiah laid the responsibility on God's shoulders when he wrote, "He giveth power to the faint; and to them that have no might he increaseth strength." (Isa. 40:29, KJV).

Peter talked of pain's temporariness and how we will endure when he wrote, "After you have suffered a little while, our God, who is full of kindness through Christ, will give you his eternal glory. He personally will come and pick you up, and set you firmly in place, and make you stronger than ever" (1 Pet. 5:10, TLB).

Did you notice that there is no mention of suffering and pain being **totally over** or completely removed, but only that Jesus will

(1) come,

(2) pick us up,

(3) set us firmly in place, and

(4) make us stronger than ever.

Knowing that our suffering is temporary and that Jesus really understands and will pick us up and make us stronger than ever challenges my heart to want to say with Mrs. Nicholson:

Oh Lord, if pain will help me to know You and Your suffering better; if pain will bring a closeness not possible in good health; if pain will give me a

creative healing ministry with other hurting people, then "press upon me further suffering," for I know the strength to endure will be mine.

In the meantime, in yesterday's mail, a dear lady wrote, "Isn't He wonderful! Stick in there, Joyce. Glory is just around the corner!" And, another letter from a Christian gentleman who had obviously experienced a great deal of pain reads,

> So may I say that I know what you are going through. I have been and will continue to pray for you.
> Remember Jesus said, "I will never leave Joyce or forsake her." (Heb. 13:5.) I felt led to put your name in.
> Sometimes people will not understand how you feel. So may I say look to Jesus for He knows and understands.

Enduring is a little more bearable with dear letters of the heart like these.

Then in today's mail, a new friend writes, "When I was having much pain, my husband gave me a tee shirt with a picture of a cat hanging onto a cross-bar, and a saying that says, 'Hang in there, Baby!' And that's what I say to you, dear one. I know the Lord will surely bless you as you continue to serve Him."

Telling someone to "hang in there, Baby!" might not sound too terribly spiritual to some of you, but to those of us in pain it translates Romans 8:17–27 and 2 Corinthians 1:3–11 into a most practical language.

While we wait with pain, we grow. Pain is an experience that is **never** wasted. Every pain is used by God and through our pain we begin to understand the meaning of communion with others, compassion for others, and sharing with Christ. And to our continued surprise, our blessings grow and we are like a field that is ready for harvest.

I do not know the author, but someone once wrote,

> Whatever, wherever I am,
> I can never be thrown away.
> If I am in sickness,
>   my sickness shall serve Him;
> In perplexity,
>   my perplexity may serve Him.
> If I am in sorrow,
>   my sorrow may serve Him.
> He does nothing in vain.
> He knows what He is about.

And I shout, "Yes, He knows what He is about and I will trust Him and hang in there!"

Chapter Four

Growing Through Obedience

To obey God in some things
and not in others,
Shows an unsound heart.
—Thomas Watson

The name of the airport's restaurant has long since blurred in my memory because there have been so many such places in my life; however, the conversation that took place there is still crystal clear.

The gifted psychologist Dr. Jim Dobson and I had just finished a three-day family seminar. We were both exhausted. If we could have poured our combined energy into a thimble, it would have barely wet the bottom. It was no time to ask Jim what made him grow spiritually; yet I was feeling a small pinch of guilt for lost opportunities in this direction. So in between bites of his chocolate fudge sundae and my stale apple pie, I said, "You know, Jim, I'm writing a book on how

Christians grow, how they mature in life, and what really makes our Christian lives productive—so, how does God help you grow?"

I think he finished his sundae because I had time to push aside my pie, pick up my pen, fold over my placemat and get all set to record his answer by the time he had reflected on my question.

Jim's life and his entire family are a personal joy to Dick and me. His books—**Dare to Discipline, Hide or Seek, What Wives Wish Their Husbands Knew About Women,** and a couple of new ones—are all being mightily used of the Lord. He is what I would call a productive, fruitful Christian gentleman.

When he finally replied he said simply, "Chastisement and obedience."

Then (I suppose because his first book was on the balance between love and discipline) he quoted a passage from the twelfth chapter of Hebrews. I came home to read that passage over and over again. I am amazed at how this Scripture has widened the window of my perspective on the inner character of God. I include much of it here because not only does it reveal the character and nature of God, but also it lays down one of the main guidelines for producing growth through chastisement and obedience.

And have you forgotten the exhortation which addresses you as sons?—"My son, do not regard lightly the discipline of the Lord, nor lose courage when you are punished by him. For the Lord disciplines him

whom he loves, and chastises every son whom he
receives."

It is for discipline that you have to endure. God is
treating you as sons; for what son is there whom his
father does not discipline?

If you are left without discipline, in which all have
participated, then you are illegitimate children and not
sons (Heb. 12:5-8, RSV).

Later in that same chapter we are told that God
disciplines us for our good so that we may share His
holiness; and then it continues, "For the moment all
discipline seems painful rather than pleasant; later it
yields the peaceful fruit of righteousness to those who
have been trained by it." (Heb. 12:11, RSV).

Evidently God is really serious when He calls us His
children, and it is His desire to see us grow into adulthood. It would also seem that He intends to train and
discipline us and that He expects us to be obedient
children.

It would be lovely if all this growing could be accomplished without rules, lessons, and growing pains, but
any thinking parent knows better.

Jim Dobson said that all through the Christian's
walk it is as if God is whispering to us, telling us about
the way that is best. Then the Lord's voice gets
stronger and louder, and finally we hear Him saying,
"This is what I want you to do; now you do it." And
then we have to make a choice. We can choose to
diligently obey or to knowingly disobey. It's up to us.

I have long surmised that all those beautiful fruits of

the Spirit—love, joy, peace, patience, kindness, good-
ness, faithfulness, gentleness, and self-control—are
all preceded by one continual procedure on our part:
obedience.

I would like to have all nine of those attributes shining in my life like large klieg lights, but I'll have none of
them if I am not willing to turn my will over to the Holy
Spirit. Without my obedience, those fruits are as remote and unobtainable as the farthest planet in space.

Obedience is tough. It is a continuing process, a
daily thing, and to obey means conforming to God's
will—**not ours.**

How often have I said, "I know what God wants me
to do in this matter, but I am not willing to do it." The
sad thing is that when those efforts of mine end in
frustrating failure, I rarely remember that it was my
deliberate choice to ignore God's will that determined the outcome.

I have taken several classes from Dr. William Glasser, M.D., and I've read most of his books; and although he does not profess to be a Christian, I see
biblical principles in his teachings and writings. A lot
of what he says boils down to what he calls the three
R's of living—

1. Do right.
2. Be real.
3. Take the responsibility.

All through the Scriptures God has laid out those
three R's, and the connecting thread always seems to
be the word **obedience.**

It takes obedience to what God says to be able to do

the right thing, say the right word, and think the right thought. It takes obedience that is willing to risk what "others think" before one can become an honest, genuine person. It also takes obedience and a disciplined commitment to Christ in everyday ethics to be able to confidently assume responsibility for our behavior.

Obedience and discipline, like emotional and physical suffering, are expensive, but they can be the greatest growing forces of our lives.

I have seen some excellent illustrations of obedience and discipline on the part of a few airplane pilots.

For the better part of ten years now my speaking schedule has been very heavy, and because of time pressures, I fly to most out-of-town engagements. I have flown overseas assignments to the Far East, Middle East, Europe, Central America, and Canada as well as to all the states in America. I've also flown in every type of air vehicle, from big wide-bodied jets, small jets, commuters, single-engine planes to large and small helicopters. Pilots of every description have taken me to my destinations, and many times they have provided me with very colorful, if not downright scary, experiences.

The qualities I like in a pilot, whether he is a captain of a 747 jet or the lone pilot of a single-engine Cessna 150, are obedience and a disciplined mind. I also want him to practice Dr. Glasser's three R's of "doing right, being real, and taking responsibility" in flying.

I'll never forget the time I learned how badly I wanted those qualities in the cockpit. I had to speak in

89

a remote California military base and when a young Christian pilot heard what a time I was having finding a commercial flight, he offered to charter a plane and fly me in.

Without checking his qualifications or his ratings and licenses (my first mistake), I eagerly jumped at the chance of flying in and out on the same evening.

I met the pilot at the airport and we climbed into the single-engine plane.

I have some fears—like my exaggerated fear of snakes and lizards—but flying is not one of them. However, because I have been flying for so many years I am very familiar with pilot and flying procedures, and I vividly remember a small shiver of fear running down my back when the young man failed to yell "prop clear" as he started the engine, didn't radio the tower for weather, and (scariest of all) did not seem to run through a visible or invisible checklist.

I buckled my seat belt and inquired, "No checklist procedure tonight?"

He smiled. His face was beaming with confidence and he tapped the side of his head as he said, "It's all in here."

"Did you file a flight plan?"

He shook his head no and winked. I wondered what on earth that meant.

There I sat strapped into that Cessna, zooming down the runway beside this bright Christian pilot who had broken every basic rule of flying before the wheels ever left the ground. Outwardly I was a picture of cool calmness, but inside my emotions were having a free-for-all riot.

I've never learned to pilot a plane simply because I love flying as a passenger. But this was one plane trip that made me wish I had taken flying lessons.

The pilot and I skimmed over the foothills and my flight experience warned me that we were entirely too close to the hills.

"Aren't we a little low?" I ventured.

Craning his neck a bit to look over the side he said, "Oh, maybe so. I'll take her up a thousand." Then he added, "If you see anything coming up on your side, let me know."

It was no more than three seconds later when I said, as controlled as possible, "How do you feel about fire trails coming up from the mountain on my side?" Then I braced myself for the crash landing that I was sure was about to take place.

He took my altitude evaluation in his stride and we climbed another few feet, avoided the crash, and flew on toward our destination.

The rest of the trip was uneventful except that my pilot kept entertaining me with a whole collection of stories about his "near miss" air disasters and landing mishaps.

At one point in his running horror report, he turned to me and said, "You are a very relaxed lady and a marvelous passenger." I smiled and thought, I didn't graduate tops in my class in drama school for nothing!

The trip going home through heavy clouds, fog, and

91

with no radio contact (until I insisted on it), made the earlier flight seem like an effortless exercise.

Silently, I began some diligent conversations with the Lord. I remember bargaining for my life by saying that if the Lord got me down safely, never, ever would I fly with someone who did not have his instrument rating or who was not willing to be **obedient** to air safety rules. The Lord kept His end of the agreement; we landed at 3:00 A.M. in an out-of-the-way town because fog had settled over Los Angeles. And since then, by the way, I've kept my part of the bargain!

I want a pilot who is not too big, too important, too experienced, or too seasoned to be obedient. I have learned that when a plane has crashed and the investigators lay the blame on "pilot error," it almost always means a pilot has disobeyed or failed to regard some long-standing, often simple rule.

If obedience to man-made rules and maintaining a disciplined routine are some of the major ways of avoiding physical injury, then obedience to God's rules and laws and keeping a disciplined mind are doubly important to our spiritual health and longevity.

After observing pilots for years, I have come to pray this prayer:

Lord, don't ever let me get so wrapped up in my own goings and comings, my own family, or even my own God-given work that I fail to heed the still, small voice of Your Spirit. Help me to hear You quickly when Your voice is just a whisper so I will not miss the direction of Your plan and end up in devastating disaster.

Abraham and Joshua are often cited as Old Testament examples of obedient servants of God; however, while those men were sterling in their unfailing obedience, I always think of someone else.

I think of Joseph, who would have made a terrific present-day pilot. He was a man of faithful obedience whose disciplined heart and mind never faltered for a moment.

I think we all tend to look admiringly at Joseph, who at the age of thirty was given the powerful job of prime minister by Egypt's Pharaoh. We are so enamored with his success, we gloss over the tumultuous growing up time the Lord allowed Joseph to endure the first thirty years of his life, and we rarely see the strength of Joseph's never-wavering obedience to God.

Read the whole story of Joseph's life in Genesis, chapters 37–50. Once you get started you will find it is one of those hard-to-put-down stories. It presents a clear, unobstructed view of the measure of a man's diligent, dedicated obedience.

Joseph could have become cynical, irreligious, and (especially in Egypt) a sensualist. But circumstances did not mar Joseph's character; rather they strengthened and prepared him for greatness.

We are told of three different occasions when Joseph could have become embittered or could have yielded to a temptation of one kind or another. First, he was sold by his brothers into slavery; then Potiphar's wife tried to seduce him; and finally, he was falsely accused and imprisoned. Yet Joseph remained steadfast and obedient to God.

A lesser man could not have borne these drastic changes of life-styles. Some men could have never gone from home to slavery to dungeons and then, at thirty years of age, to a palace to become one of the greatest men in all of Egypt and second only to the king.

How did Joseph bear his ugly childhood and his later life, which were laced with lies and deception? Joseph endured these traumatic happenings because he understood that **everything** in life has meaning. He knew that even mistakes and misunderstandings have meaning, and so Joseph **chose** to be obedient to God. He coped with the adversities of his life with a moral rightness and a right state of mind.

He probably did not **feel** obedient after his brothers left him to die down in the pit; nor did he **feel** obedient when he was sold into slavery; and he probably didn't **feel** obedient when he was framed and sent to prison. But obedience was a methodically planned move of his will. He chose obedience.

In respect for his obedience, God gave Joseph the sensitivity to see the proper priority of prisons and palaces; and so, in return for Joseph's unfailing obedience, the Lord gave him immense security amidst all the changes of his life. The Scripture says, "The Lord was with Joseph." (Gen. 39:21, KJV).

Joseph disciplined his mind with strict obedience and learned the lessons of the soul. By obeying God he learned how to rule; and when the great moment came, Joseph stepped from prison into the most prominent position a ruler could have—and he was already seasoned and highly skilled for the challenge.

Had Joseph remained at home, a favorite son of his father, or returned there at some point in time or had Potiphar not thrown him into prison, he would not have been the prime minister of Egypt. But Joseph's whole life was one of obedience. It started with his obeying God first—then his father, employer, jailer, and eventually the king of Egypt.

Joseph was obedient during setbacks, delays, and even while sitting on the sidelines watching someone else carry the ball. He understood that God's delays are a part of our spiritual education, for in waiting we learn to develop our faith and trust. Joseph knew, too, that to **accept** the circumstances God sends, though their usefulness or purpose is not understood, is true obedience and submission to the will of God.

Had Joseph not chosen to be an obedient son of God, he never would have been the deliverer of the Egyptian people nor of his own family; nor could he have been the instrument and channel to fulfill God's promise and purpose.

Like Joseph, most of us desire some form of power, talents, usefulness, or blessings in this life; but what we need is a measure of Joseph's concept of unfailing obedience and untiring discipline to sustain us in the midst of overwhelming adversities and puzzling, frustrating events.

Just this year in my own life, I have tripped over the word **obedience** several times, and lately I've been running smack into the "obedience" wall.

I can hear Jim Dobson saying, "The Lord says,

'This is what I want you to do, now you do it.' " But not too long ago my level of disciplined obedience seemed to be running low.

At the first of this year, my jaw pain was acting up more than usual. If the Lord wasn't going to heal it just now, I felt I should give up all singing and public speaking. The price was too high—speaking and having it followed by such acute pain was simply not worth it.

I could hear the Lord's veto, but it was only whispered, and so I ignored it.

About the time I thought I had definitely reached a decision not to take any more engagements, I had to fulfill a long-standing booking at Robert Schuller's church in Garden Grove, California. I reluctantly went, and from the first four bars of my beginning song and on into my talk and the luncheon that followed, my jaw and entire head pounded into an explosion of pain.

Even as I spoke I mentally said, "This is it! I'm not going to go on taking this pain."

The still, small voice said, "This is what I want you to do—now do it." I closed my ears and finished speaking—grateful that it was over.

When I sat down, Jeenie, one of my secretaries, handed me a note. It was from a dear lady wanting to know if we would like to meet Corrie ten Boom. I scribbled back that yes I would, if it was not an imposition. But privately I wondered if I could endure the pain long enough to even see Corrie—much less meet and converse with her.

After the luncheon, with my head still violently

throbbing, we went to meet that beautiful Dutch saint.

I must say that I didn't go see Corrie ten Boom that warm, spring afternoon in order to grow by the method of obedience. I simply went with my secretary and her friend to meet and enjoy Corrie. How differently it all worked out.

When I entered Corrie's room, she was lying in bed, all propped up by pillows and wearing a frilly eyelet-edged pink and blue housecoat.

"I'm not sick—just resting," the eighty-four-year-old beauty hastened to assure me.

Her shining white hair formed a literal halo around her face. The pink in her cheeks was the exact shade of pink in her housecoat, and her blue eyes danced a continuous jig of joy. Even though pain was blurring my vision, I remember thinking that I had never seen anyone so incredibly beautiful, nor had I been so close and within touching range of Jesus as I was then.

Corrie's presence in that room would have been a heady experience in itself, but the presence of Jesus was a little more than overwhelming. She motioned for us to sit down, but I felt like Moses must have felt before the Lord on holy ground and I wished I could remove my shoes. However, when I remembered the small hole my toenail had made in my hose, I compromised and did the next best thing—I remained standing.

"Joyce, why are you standing?" she asked. I was afraid she wouldn't buy my Moses-on-holy-ground theory, and so I mumbled something about not wanting to tire her. I was graciously told to sit down.

97

I did.

We talked of many things.

Years ago Corrie had spoken at my father's church in Reseda, California, just a few months before my mother died. Corrie's long-standing acquaintanceship with the ways of dying caused her to clearly see death's shadow hovering over my mother, and in their first moment of meeting, Corrie said to my mother, "Oh, I see you are going to heaven soon."

My sister tells me that my mother nodded yes and Corrie continued, "When you see Betsy and Father, tell them I said hello and that I send my love."

I'm sure my mother kept her promise a few months later, and I had always wanted to thank Corrie for the gentle way she encouraged my mother's walk across the bridge of death.

That afternoon, too, we talked of Corrie's newest books, of her little tape recorder laying by her pillow; and then, in a way not known or practiced by many Christian celebrities, she straightened up, looked directly at me and said, "Now, that's enough about me. Tell me about Joyce Landorf and your books."

I was deeply touched by her lack of self-centeredness and her genuine interest in someone else. My pain was numbing my ability to speak very well, but I managed to tell her of my teen-age rebellion to God and the church, my mother's prayers, my disastrous marriage to Dick, our suicide attempts, and finally, our conversion and our life now in Christ.

Corrie shook her head, leaned forward in her bed, and said with a bright enthusiasm, "Just think, Joyce, your mother's prayers are still being answered now—years after her death—and God is really using you!"

It might have been right then, or just a little later, but suddenly I could not hear Corrie or the voices of those around me—only the still, small voice of the Lord, which by this time was through with whispering. And I clearly heard, "Corrie endured months in various prisons, and years at Hitler's Ravensbruck Concentration Camp, yet she was obedient to Me. Joyce, **what is a jaw ache?**" I had to answer, "Nothing, Lord, compared to that."

And I went home crying and saying, "Yes, Lord. I'll continue. I may not be able to sing as many songs or speak at as many places, but I will **continue to obey you** and I will not count the cost as exorbitant but appropriate."

Aristotle said, "Wicked men obey from fear, good men from love."

The kind of obedience God wants from us should not be motivated out of a frightened or intimidated spirit, but out of our love.

Jesus Himself called us to obedience: "If you **love** me, obey me" (John 14:15, TLB, emphasis mine).

When Moses was explaining to the Israelites the importance of keeping God's commandments, he promised, "If you obey them they will give you a reputation for wisdom and intelligence" (Deut. 4:6, TLB). Then, in order to encourage them to **continue** in obedience, he instructed the men to "Be very careful never to forget what you have seen God doing for you. May his miracles have a deep and permanent effect upon your lives! Tell your children and your grandchildren about the glorious miracles he did" (Deut. 4:9, TLB).

Since Dick and I have just recently become grandparents, this verse has taken on a new glow; and even though our little grandbaby, April Joy, is only eight months old, I caught her grandpa whispering in her ear the other day about how good God is and how He's blessed her.

Moses, a real and practical man, knew there would be terribly hard days and times of deep affliction for his people, but majestically he added this glorious promise—a promise given in reward for obedience:

> When thou art in tribulation, and all these things are come upon thee, even in the latter days, if thou turn to the Lord thy God, and shalt be obedient unto his voice; (For the Lord thy God is a merciful God;) He will not forsake thee, neither destroy thee, nor forget the covenant of thy fathers which he sware unto them (Deut. 4:30,31, KJV).

So our obedience is rewarded by God, and this verse tells us God will not forsake, destroy, or forget us, in our daily growing process, if we practice obedient living.

Clearly I can hear, "This is what I want you to do—now you do it."

And I have to answer, "Yes, Lord."

Chapter Five

Growing Through Belonging

In the triangle of love between ourselves,
God, and other people is found the secret
of existence and the best foretaste, I
suspect, that we can have on earth of what
heaven will probably be like.
                            —Samuel M. Shoemaker

We exist and live in a society that plunges head long into the race to **belong.** We want desperately to be accepted, we want to belong. We buy memberships into everything from tennis and country clubs to discount and wholesale stores. Yet, when it comes to belonging to the body of Christ, there are still many people and groups of people who insist on going it alone like some kind of Christian lone ranger.

I have looked into more than a few tanned, wind-burned teen-age faces and heard words like these: "I can worship God on my surfboard a lot better than in some stuffy traditional church."

Equally as many times I have met people who attend a "closed" church.

I remember once talking with a dedicated Christian businessman who was seated next to me on a plane. He poured out his troubled heart in regard to his terrible uneasiness over the lack of vision in his church. While he loved the people and the pastor, his main question to me was: "Do you think God is leading me out of such a church?"

The membership of the church was limited to about fifty people who had no outreach program to non-Christians in the community. The meetings were three to four hours long, with lots of good congregational singing. The sermons did not vary or change in topics or words over the years. The church's social life consisted of a midweek dinner and other than that the members were not encouraged to be friends with any outsider or to go anywhere else.

There was never any special meeting for the youth; nor was there any summer program for children such as daily vacation Bible school. When I asked what the budget was for home and foreign missions, the man shook his head sadly and said, "We have no missionary budget or outreach whatsoever."

In his words, his whole church-life experience boiled down to "getting together to get a blessing."

The surfer with his I'll-do-it-my-own-way spirit and the businessman who belongs to a church with restricted tunnel vision are at opposite ends of the poles in their methods, but both are missing the same thing—God's most unique method of teaching us to become giants in a land of spiritual and moral dwarfs.

We grow corporately. A great church **can** be an avenue to our learning and it **can** lead us into living stable, unshakeable lives if we recognize its potential and seek the church of God's choice for us.

Paul wrote to the church in Corinth about their joining together to be members of one body and at one point said: "Now here is what I am trying to say: All of you together are the one body of Christ and each one of you is a separate and necessary part of it" (1 Cor. 12:27, TLB).

To the Ephesians, Paul said we "belong in God's household with every other Christian" (Eph. 2:19, TLB). Paul never described the process of being a Christian as a game played unilaterally. He always referred to this process as a thing we do **together** via team work.

To the surfer, I would have to admit that worshiping God in nature's beautiful seascape of waves and foam can be done, at least to some degree, but God's creation of all nature is only one small dimension of God's creativity. Our God is not limited to creating lovely beaches, mountains, and other majestic scenic beauties. He has many other sides and His abilities are like hundreds of lights refracted into a thousand different angles. To see God in only one area, the area of His material creations, is to miss the magnificent wholeness of God.

Our God is not only the Creator of all life, but He is our Sovereign King, our Savior, Shepherd, and the God of forgiveness, mercy, and salvation. You don't quite get all that shooting curls on a surfboard or relaxing on sun-drenched beaches. Besides, the surfer out there on his board is ignoring a very important principle—that of belonging to a group of believers.

The Scriptures tell us not to forsake the assembling of ourselves together and for good reason. We need collective fellowship, comfort, and encouragement.

Even a surfer gets off his board at one time or another, and as he relaxes on the beach, guess what he does? He talks with other surfers about their mutual passion for surfing until they all return to the water to surf. As with any group of like-minded people, it's called "collective fellowship." People really do need people.

Paul wrote, "We who believe are carefully joined together with Christ as parts of a beautiful, constantly growing temple for God" (Eph. 2:21, TLB).

To think we can grow, blossom, and bloom separately is not only ridiculous but highly frustrating in this stress-and-trauma-filled world.

I'm sure this is why Paul encouraged us to "talk with each other **much** about the Lord, quoting psalms and hymns and singing sacred songs, making music in your hearts to the Lord" (Eph. 5:19, TLB, emphasis mine). He knew we would need all the loving encouragement of belonging that we could get.

My strongest words to the surfer would be just this: whenever a believer habitually or by principle removes himself from belonging to a body of other believers, he ends up a defeated, often bitter loser.

I personally know men and women who became disillusioned with "belonging to the body of believers," and for one reason or another left the church. They went off to do their own thing and said, "I'll worship God in my own way"; or they used the tired old cliché, "I believe in God—in here," as they thumped their chests with a smug pride or winked their eyes with a look of secret wisdom.

As I have watched their lives over the years, all I have seen is the ignorance of their decision and the brokenness that is reflected in the lives of their entire family.

Henry Ward Beecher once said, "The church is not a gallery for the exhibition of eminent Christians, but a school for the education of imperfect ones."

What better place can we learn about
   the kind of love that comes from really caring,
   the freedom from guilt that comes with God's forgiveness,
   the joys of giving that come with stewardship, or
   the unsurpassed empathy and comfort that come out of hearts eager to please God?

What better arena for real lessons than in a godly church?

The church, when led by the Holy Spirit and full of believers who are committed to the "triangle of love" among ourselves, God, and all others in the world today, is a healthy, beautifully growing body—a real place of learning.

To the businessman and other people who belong to a "closed church," I would have to concede that drawing together in a tight, elite circle of like minds, praising God, singing hymns, and taking no responsibility for any sinner outside would probably produce a euphoric sense of well-being and spiritual security. However, one of the greatest dangers would be the formation of a thick cloud of spiritual pride that would blind their eyes to the need for inner growth and certainly to the need for taking action on Jesus' Great Commission.

The writer of Acts quoted Jesus as saying, "But when the Holy Spirit has come upon you, you will receive power to testify about me with great effect, to the people in Jerusalem, throughout Judea, in Samaria, and to the ends of the earth, about my death and resurrection" (Acts 1:8, TLB).

So to stay safely locked into a closed church means that the Good News will never reach the sidewalk in front of the church much less the town around it. The cloistered closed church violates our commitment to Spirit-led witnessing, and our growing potential reaches its saturation point very quickly. Spiritually, we die off right in the pew.

Isolated monasteries and convents never really caught on because the men and women who retreated there tried to get **out** of this world rather than **into** it as Christ commanded.

If it is true that we grow through belonging to a Christ-centered church, one that reaches out to the surrounding community and world, then it is equally true that we need Christian friends.

Again, we grow corporately.

Psalm 1:1 tells us that a man is blessed who does not walk in the counsel of the ungodly. That verse implies that when we need advice and counsel, we should seek it only from godly people.

If we have to live this life, which at times can be pretty gruesome, God has given us several ways to endure, and certainly one of them is the valued love and advice of a godly friend.

The Scriptures are full of admonishments for us to be a friend and to make friends. Joseph Joubert said, "If we spend our lives loving, we will have no leisure to complain or feel unhappiness."

It seems that the first Christians spent a good deal of time learning how to love each other and become friends. Romans 12:10 tells us about "brotherly love"; Galatians 2:9 talks of the "right hands of fellowship"; Hebrews 13:1, of brotherly love again; and 1 John 4:20, 21 really comes down hard on the importance of loving our brothers. It says,

> If anyone says "I love God," but keeps on hating his brother, he is a liar; for if he doesn't love his brother who is right there in front of him, how can he love God whom he has never seen? And God himself has said that one must love not only God, but his brother too (1 John 4:20,21, TLB).

I have recently developed a new perspective on this business of growing through belonging and cultivating

Christian friends. When I did the research for my biblical novel about Martha, **I Came to Love You Late,** I was fascinated by the types of people who were drawn to Jesus. I found that whole groups of people were drawn to Him by His magnetic charisma. He was always accompanied by smaller groups of believing followers, His dedicated disciples, and those disciples who chose to be especially close to Him. But the Bible records Jesus as having three special friends: Martha, Mary, and Lazarus.

It was to his friends' house that Jesus came to rest, eat, and at times retreat. I find it interesting that Jesus, the Son of God, needed human companionship. He made regular visits to their home, ate and conversed with them, and as the Scriptures tell us, He dearly loved these friends.

Was Jesus not, in fact, setting down a living example of a principle and commandment He had taught publicly? The commandment to love one another is the beginning of growing together through belonging, and if Jesus Himself needed to belong, how much more must we?

The verse in John where Jesus gives us the commandment to love one another is followed immediately by a very interesting statement. Jesus says, "Your strong love for each other will prove to the world that you are my disciples" (John 13:35, TLB).

My dear friend Keith Korstjens was talking about the marital problems he deals with each day as a counselor and pastor, and at one point in his conversation he said, "You know, Joyce, the more I talk and counsel with people, the more I am convinced that in every relationship we either **actively create love** or we **actively destroy love.**"

The Christian has a choice again. He can create or destroy love in any relationship. If he chooses to **create** loving bonds, then he is giving the world the best proof of his Christianity. He must reach out, embrace others, and **create** friendships.

Not only does growing through belonging happen by our attending a Spirit-led church and cultivating friends, but it also happens through discipleship. There are two areas, or rather time frames, when we need the fine tuning of discipling.

The first time for discipling, that is, being a teachable student, comes right after our conversion to Christ.

We need to continue on with the parent, pastor, or person who introduced us to Christ and who is our spiritual father or mother. I cannot stress too much the value of staying and learning from those who are more spiritually mature. We need their spiritual "shepherdship" and guidance until we are ready to move from the milk stage of babyhood into the meaty sessions of adulthood.

When Dick and I became Christians, no one actually helped us in a step-by-step fashion to accept Christ. Many people had prayed for us, but we were alone and separated from human contact when we invited Christ into our lives. However, the need for discipling was very great and God placed us rather quickly in the right church and Dr. Ted Cole, our pastor, became our

109

teacher and discipler. Both Dick and I took notes on each sermon or Sunday school class our pastor taught, and we continued that procedure for over three exciting "baby Christian" years.

Pete Gillquist was led to the Lord years ago by Ray Nethery, and in Pete's words, "As I look back, had I not relied heavily on Ray Nethery's wisdom and insight to help guide my decisions in life, no telling where I'd be." Both Dick and I can say that same thing about our pastor's wisdom and viable Christ-centered discipling.

John Randolph once wrote,

> I believe I should have been swept away by the flood of French infidelity, if it had not been for one thing: the remembrance of the time when my sainted mother used to make me kneel by her side, taking my little hands in hers, and caused me to repeat the Lord's Prayer.

His mother's first efforts in discipling her son left their marks, and John Randolph grew into godly manhood.

The second time frame for lessons on discipleship comes during our continued daily process as a **maturing** Christian. I said "maturing"—not "matured"—because I believe the process is never-ending. Even people such as the sainted Corrie ten Boom, believe it or not, are still in the process of maturing, ripening, and becoming God's people.

When I asked Pete Gillquist how he grows spiritually, now that he's a maturing Christian, he answered,

110

"I grow because of four times a year." Then he explained that four times a year he gets together with six Spirit-led friends for a week at a time to pray, share, encourage, debate, and even correct each other. They put themselves under the authority of God and each other, and the lovely, yet strenuous work of discipling goes on—hot and heavy, but productive!

We all need that friend or set of friends who can critique our Christian efforts from a **loving** perspective. I hasten to say though that I don't know **anyone** who can take flat-out criticism, even when it's disguised by the thin veil of "I tell you this in Christian love." But all of us need a timely critique, an update, or a course correction from time to time. It seems to me that one of the most ideal and practical ways of changing our direction or of keeping on God's right-on course is Pete's four-times-a-year plan.

It will not be easy to find the people, place, or time to put yourself into such a plan; but, if you want to badly enough, you can find people and places, and you will **take** or **make** time.

Years ago I circled all the "I wills" in several Psalms, and I read one in Psalm 119 just yesterday. David said, "I will"; he **made up his mind.** I doubt the "I will" decision was a snap one or easily done.

I wanted to put this principle of reevaluation into practice, and so I've just arranged to spend a few days with my friend Clare Bauer. I will be tired from my speaking engagements in Michigan, but I'm going to take all those crazy flights to Idaho before coming back to my home in California anyway. Clare and I both need the lovely work of discipling that God always seems to do in our lives when we are together.

One last thing growing through belonging gives us is a new feeling of togetherness brought on by a united effort. I am particularly aware of this in the lives of Christian women everywhere I go.

Perhaps this has happened significantly in the last five years because of the enormous pressure brought about by women's lib groups. Today's woman is hearing a thousand different drum beats that tell her who she is supposed to be, what she is supposed to feel, and how she is supposed to succeed.

At first, I think Christian women panicked and for good reason. It seemed the main message of the women's movement was: "You're dumb if you are satisfied with being a wife, mother, and homemaker." From every form of media available, the Christian woman got the impression that everyone was in step but her. Little by little, however, Christian women began seeking out other Christian women, and the bonds of Christian love began to strengthen.

I get quite annoyed when the women's liberation spokespersons say they speak for **all women.** They don't speak for me, nor do they speak for thousands of Christian women all over the world. But for a while we were all intimidated into thinking that to be a Christian woman meant being very elderly, very weird, very much a malcontent who needs a crutch, or a combination of all three.

But our panic was short-lived because, little by little,

Christian women began seeking out other Christian women, and they began banding together in many different ways and in all sorts of areas.

They came together in the traditional ways of
- Bible study groups,
- prayer groups, and
- koinonia groups

They also began to gather at public functions like
- day-long family seminars,
- weekend retreats for women, and
- weekly classes on inner and outer Christian beauty.

But most amazing of all is the way thousands of Christian women have united together in a quiet, rather private way like
- Two neighborhood women who share Christ over coffee,
- Six to twelve women who pray together in a prayer chain (I have twelve of the most precious from our church who pray regularly for me in a prayer chain. I call them the "all-the-difference-in-the-world bunch" because that's exactly how my schedule and ministry has improved since they have been my prayer partners this year), and
- Individual women who are reading not only their Bibles but also the tremendous Christian books on the market today.

In all of this, the Christian women around the world are the fastest growing group of people I know.

My brother-in-law and sister are pastoring a church in Michigan. Here is part of a letter from one of the great Christian gals in that church. She has a lot to say about growing through belonging.

> I'm a member of Central Wesleyan where Pastor Paul and Marilyn are ministering to us beautifully. I love them very much already.
>
> Lately I'm learning more and more what it really means to be part of God's family together, and parts of His body.
>
> Because I've read your books, and now because I know of you through Paul and Marilyn, I'm prompted to write.
>
> I'm becoming more and more aware of the beautiful, God-gifted people around me, and I am learning to recognize and appreciate them as such. I appreciate your ministry through your books, music, and speaking ability because I see Christ fulfilling Himself through you—your talents and skills—and I am seeing the "beauty of Jesus" in you, with grace and charm the world doesn't show. I just wanted you to know I'm thankful for you today.
>
> Then, also, because I know you are struggling with a physical problem, I'm praying for you. I recognize that it's my "responsibility and privilege" to pray for you, as my sister in Christ, which brings peace of heart and a thankful spirit according to Colossians 3:15.
>
> Today, I pray that the Holy Spirit will encourage and love you in a way that you'll experience the joy of our Lord.
>
> In Christian love,
> Phyl

She names three definite areas of growth:
(1) learning what it means to be a part of God's family,

114

(2) becoming aware of others and recognizing and appreciating them, and

(3) realizing her responsibilities as a Christian woman.

How beautifully she is growing. Yet, she is only one of thousands of Christian women who are learning the joys of belonging to God's family.

There are many alert and bright-eyed women who are taking the baton of the relay race of life and running to win! Enjoy Paul's words, even though he wrote them so long ago: "Now you are no longer strangers to God and foreigners to heaven, but you are members of God's very own family, citizens of God's country, and you **belong** in God's household with every other Christian" (Eph. 2:19, TLB, emphasis mine).

Chapter Six

Growing Through the Three D's

God asks no man whether he will accept life.
That is not the choice.
You must take it.
The only choice is **How.**

—Henry Ward Beecher

I can think of three words, all beginning with the letter "d" that describe potential sources of growing. I say "potential sources of growing" because often we refuse to accept these sources as ways for God to mold our lives and to cause us to mature.

The first "d" word is "differences." Believe it or not, we can grow through our differences. We need not be horrified that somebody butters his toast, parks his car, or combs his hair differently from us. We need not be "grieved in our spirits" because so-and-so has deliberately chosen a spiritual position that is not up to

117

our prescribed image. In fact, those differences may be the very way God leads us into acceptance and tolerance.

Each time I hear one Christian criticizing or judging another Christian's spiritual progress, their church affiliation, or their denominational practices, I am reminded of a rather simple yet clear analogy.

Not five minutes from my home is a large and beautiful shopping center. It is an enclosed mall arrangement, surrounded by acres of parking lots, and it boasts of over two hundred fine, quality stores. With excellent management and maintenance, lots of foot traffic, and artistically planned indoor landscaping, the center is enjoying a very profitable operation.

I do not think all two hundred stores are "super" or "fantastic" as their ads indicate; in fact, I don't shop in a lot of them. Yet nothing but lack of time stops me from being one of the center's best customers.

Just yesterday, I added up all the dress shops, on one of the large directory boards. Not counting four large major department stores, there were fifty specialty shops that sell women's clothes exclusively.

Although all these stores offer women's garments, each caters to a particular age group, size, type, or style. Out of fifty stores, I'm interested in shopping in only five or six. My twenty-two-year-old daughter Laurie, who kids me about the fact that she wouldn't be caught dead in one of those "older-lady shops," buys her clothes in five or six different stores.

But we both go to the center and have a marvelous time together. We shop or browse and neither of us thinks it is "just awful" about those other forty or so stores whose doors we never darken.

Also, we would never dream of going into those unpatronized stores to seek out the managers or some saleslady, and "in love" tell them how far wrong their buyer has gone or how they should spruce up their store or merchandise.

But Christians are super serious about their differences. This was abruptly pointed out once when a friend of mine gave me a very hard time over the church we attend. I asked him, "Why can't you accept me as a born-again child of God, just as I have accepted you—as a believer?"

He got very agitated and shouted, "Because Jesus is coming back again very soon, and you and everybody in THAT church are going to hell, that's why!"

I am deeply saddened by the lack of love and unity between believers and by remarks like this one from my well-meaning friend. When are we going to stop shooting our poison arrows into other Christians who are firm and solid in their faith, but who do not cross their t's and dot their i's in our specifically prescribed ways?

There seems to be some kind of holy crusade going on between so many Christians. The hot or cold wars are rather endless—

- between excited, enthusiastic charismatics and dyed-in-the-wool, stanch noncharismatics.
- between sprinkled Presbyterians, immersed Baptists, and those who believe water baptism is essential for salvation.

I'm Still Growing

- between rigidly proud "straight" people and deliberately "loose" counterculture groups.
- between left- and right-wing believers, and even between those who embrace the Bible's new translations (including paraphrased versions) and those who read **only** King James.

We Christians may not see eye to eye on these and other issues in the church, but certainly, in the name of common sense and Christian maturity, we should be able to walk in unity without waging war on one another.

In his profoundly great and disturbing book **Let's Quit Fighting About the Holy Spirit,** Pete Gillquist tells of a delightful fantasy conversation between two men who lived in Jesus' day and who were both healed of blindness. As the story goes, two men got to comparing notes one day about their healings and they discovered Jesus was the healer in both cases.

Next, they discussed the method and technique of Jesus' healing and to their dismay, they discovered that Jesus used an instant-type procedure to heal one; but with the other, He used a totally different mud-on-the-eyes approach.

Both men were frustrated, but positive of one thing: Jesus could not possibly have used the "other" method to heal. In great disbelief, one man says to the other man, "There's no way it could have happened like that!" And then Pete's punch line follows: "And there you have it, folks. The start of the world's first

120

two denominations. The Mudites and the Anti-Mudites."

Some of us are terribly busy being in one camp or the other. We have long since forgotten that the Scriptures call us over and over again to a ministry of love. But mostly we have forgotten that mature growing Christians make allowances for each other, forbear one another in love, and remain loyal at all costs.

In the fourth chapter of Ephesians, Paul practically begged the Christians of Ephesus to act and walk in a manner that would be appropriate to their calling. Then he wrote, "Be humble and gentle. Be patient with each other, making allowance for each other's faults because of your love" (Eph. 4:2, TLB). The King James Version reads, ". . . forbearing one another in love."

In other words, there are many splendid opportunities in our relationships with other Christians when we should simply shut up, put up, forbear, or make allowances because of our love! My secretary, Brenda, made this comment when she read this book in its rough draft form: "Why does there have to be so much competition? We're all on the same team!" It is our Christian responsibility to stop making a federal case out of our nit-picking differences, and allow God to teach us some sober maturity.

Your worship service may be conducted in a totally different way from mine, your theology and life-style may differ considerably from mine, and your goals or priorities may be worlds apart from mine; but both of us had better remember that the only unpardonable sin in heaven or on earth is rejecting Jesus as Lord and Savior.

One difference that rankles and repulses Christian men and women the most in our society today is the ancient sin of homosexuality. There's nothing new about homosexuality—it existed in ancient Greece and Rome—and Paul, bless his courageous heart, dealt with it when he was on earth.

I suspect with today's emphasis on "coming out of the closet" and "doing your own thing," we will tend to think that sexual sin is more widespread today, and that there are more sexual deviates than in years past. Actually, we are simply **hearing** more about it. It's been here a long time.

Since even the psychiatrists and psychology experts are divided on causes and treatment for the homosexual, I was thrilled this year to see the Melodyland Church in Anaheim, California, add EXIT (Ex-gay Intervention Team) to its Hot Line Center. Their program is headed by two former homosexuals, and their work is being uniquely blessed of God. They work from the premise that homosexuality is sin, but that God can deliver a person from it. The center helps the homosexual live a straight but abundant life in Christ, and it gives its prayerful support to new men and women in Christ much like Alcoholics Anonymous does for the alcoholic.

To most of us though, we are too repulsed by the sin to show any compassion or to lovingly deal with the homosexual. We seem to be far better at accepting those who have committed violent crimes, even to the point of supporting a prison chaplain ministry, than we are at accepting the homosexual sinner.

I am deeply convicted about my own attitudes, especially when I read about the way Jesus handled the prostitute, the adulterer, and even the common thief on the cross. He did not pull Himself away from sinners in a don't-touch-me-because-you-are-unclean gesture; He did not get angry and shake them by their garments; He did not hold them up as examples of sin for the world to see; nor did He say, "How could you **do** such a thing?"

Never, not even once, did He put down the sinner with verbal condemnation. But in each case the sinner knew the extent, depth, and seriousness of his own sin and in repentance, experienced the loving forgiveness of God Himself.

I will never be a lesbian—just as I will never be a murderer—for these are not my sins. However, I must never forget that I am a sinner saved by God's grace. How dare any of us condemn or criticize the sin of others or hold ourselves up as paragons of virtue when we feel we've been rescued from the sea of sin and now sit safely in our little boats of forgiveness.

My straight life is vastly different from a gay life, but I pray God develops in me a real and honest love toward those who are most different from me; in fact, I want the kind of love that Christ showed to broken people around Him when He was here.

We will never mature in Christ if we spend our energies and time preaching **against** sinners. We must give our efforts to **lovingly dealing** with the sin and get on to the business of healing.

I am aware that some of you may violently disagree with what I have just written, but I pray that you ask God to make the last several paragraphs a time of learning or a time of examining your own soul.

But that's the problem with differences—sometimes they grow too big to overcome.

Last week I got a red hot letter from a Christian lady who took real issue with me for something I had written in my column for the "Power for Living" Sunday school paper. She definitely did not agree with me and so she wrote a long letter filled with Scripture to back up her claims about how wrong, wrong, wrong I was.

I answered her in the only way possible: "Isn't it wonderful that in Christ we have the lovely freedom to disagree?"

Most of us need to learn that we can be brothers and sisters in Christ without being identical twins.

It is uniquely true, and only true of real Christians, that there is a unity through diversity. It **is** possible through Christ!

The second "d" word can be used as mightily as the first one. It is "daily." Did you know we can grow from current events and daily newspapers, magazines and, even from the six o'clock news? It's true, but most Christians do not want to use this means for growth because if something in the news media really reaches us it usually stirs up concern and we are motivated into **acting** or **doing** something.

124

Growing Through the Three D's

This seems to be true even when we are talking about Christian periodicals, magazines, and media efforts. For instance, the **Los Angeles Times** ran a story that said that a Christian newspaper had suspended its publication after two million dollars had been invested in it. The publisher issued a statement in the final edition explaining: "Many Christians are not really interested in keeping up with the news events affecting Christian life, church, and society. There seems to be an avoidance of knowing, probably because knowing challenges us to do—and many of us are not ready for that challenge."*

We like staying away from daily challenges, yet the New Testament tells us to be good, obedient citizens—yes, even to paying our dues to the tax collector. From a biblical standpoint, our conduct in the community around us should be one of alertness, sensitivity, and responsibility. Christians who demean and criticize the media, the newspapers, and the news magazines become isolationists who shut off growth and challenges and simply stagnate in their own apathetic pool of indifference.

Once when I was speaking at a writers' conference, the small group of would-be authors were asked what in their lives contributed the most to their writing abilities, or what was the main source of inspiration for their writing.

Several writers shared, and their answers involved everything from God's direct words and inspiration, or

*Los Angeles Times, Sept. 3, 1977.

some tragic or painful incident, to the inspiration and education given by a gifted Christian teacher or a godly mother or father.

Then one woman stood and said that her inspiration came from reading and looking at **nothing** but the Bible. She went on to say that she did not watch or own a television set; she did not subscribe to a newspaper or any secular or Christian magazine; nor did she read any books because most of that "stuff," she said, was "ungodly and unnecessary." Her voice swelled with pride as she related how many hours a day she read the Bible and how awful newspapers were and how sinful it was to watch television.

I don't know what's happened to the lady in the years since that conference, but I do know she has missed out on the viable world around her and in doing so has never felt the thrill of challenges nor seen the power of God at work here on this earth. I imagine that her writing will be a bit irrelevant.

How can we ever open up our hearts to love, minister, and witness in the small corner of the world we live in if we refuse to open our ears to the crying around us and our minds and hearts to people's needs?

I believe one way to enlarge our capacity for caring and learning is by reading the daily and weekly accounts of the society, community, and world around us.

The newspapers, magazines, and six o'clock news put us in touch with the reality of life. We may not like what we find out; we may find it extremely disagreeable, even sinful, but the media can bring people and their needs to our attention. Someone once said the church is not a hotel for saints but a hospital for sinners, and so it is with Christians. We are not left on earth to relax and collect unemployment but to work, seeing to the spiritual and physical needs of the world around us. We are told to work, for the night is coming; yet some of us have been so cooped up in our own little houses that we are blissfully unaware of the approaching evening shadows or the broken lives on our block. The newspaper and media can put this into a realistic focus for us, and quite quickly.

I read the **Los Angeles Times** each day in addition to my Bible and two devotional books. I see that paper as one giant Wednesday night prayer request sheet!

Look at my newspaper today. On page 1, the right-hand column lead story seems to indicate that our President is going to need a super-human amount of wisdom if he is to handle this week's White House crisis. The press is saying, "The President's honeymoon with the country is definitely over," and so this man—the highest governing person in the United States—needs as much prayer support from Christians as he can possibly get.

On the second page is a story about a young man reared in a strong, loving Catholic family who grew up to depart from his parents' training and to eventually become a spy for some other country. Now he is sentenced to forty years in prison, and he and his family are devastated by this. I don't know them, but from all the article says of the boy and his family, they must be in deep shock. It is safe to assume that at some point in time they will desperately try to figure out just where their faith failed them, or how God fits into all of this, or how they will survive the loss and humiliation. They must be floundering in their sea of questions even while I read this account, and so I stop and ask the Lord to somehow lead them and mend their shattered souls and fragmented dreams.

On page 4 is an interesting story that tells about seventeen hundred people in the Russian city of Gorki who signed a petition asking the government to reopen one of the city's closed churches. The article goes on to say that ten years ago a similar petition drive met with threats and reprisals from the authorities. Nine of the most active participants lost their jobs and one leader was threatened with incarceration in a mental asylum. My gut-level feeling tells me these Russian citizens are my brothers and sisters and I need to hold them dearly and lovingly before the Lord today.

On page 17 is the story of famine and disease in the Mideast. It helps me respect the stew that's simmering on my stove, and my thank-you prayer at the table is not memorized and glibly mouthed but genuine.

The sports section, which I barely skim, reminds me afresh that my sports-fan husband is out of town on a business trip and is working on a tough assignment. I stop and pray for the needy sports fans he works with and ask God to give him "journeying mercies."

The women's section has a large feature story, spread across the top half of the paper on a leading women's rights leader. The glowing article tells about all the triumphs of this year's resolutions and achievements. The piece, covering more space than the paper would ever allow for a report on a Christian convention or seminar, is accompanied by a big picture of the activist/editor/speaker who is shown smiling and raising her clenched fist.

The whole report challenged me, broke my heart, and made me dedicate myself anew to ministering to women. The women's movement pictured on the women's page today alerts me that it's time we of the silent majority spoke up to say: We will not be put down because of our faith or slandered because of the biblical principles we live by. We will be, to the best of our abilities, the women God wants us to be. To be that woman means experiencing the true meaning of freedom and joy!

The theater and TV section, with its sensational movie captions and its descriptions of television shows, which must come across like drawn-out dirty jokes, was a marvelous contrast to the Bible and the books **Knowing God** and **A Touch of Wonder** I am reading each morning.

I put the paper down, thankful and rejoicing that I belong to the Lord Jesus Christ and His church instead of to the world. I also know and understand the world around me a little better; and while much of what I read was discouraging and painted dark pictures above the sound of the world's drums, I could hear the steady beating of God's voice saying,

Be still and know I am God—

> Be not afraid—
> I will never leave you—
> Will you take the Great Commission?
> Will you feed my sheep?
> Do you care?

Once more my daily newspaper shoved and pushed me into praying and caring and, above all, into growing.

Before I leave the discussion of the word **daily,** I want to write about one other aspect of the word. I am quite sure that just as God teaches us through the big important issues and crises of life, He also is perfectly capable of teaching us through daily little episodes which—while they are not earthshaking—do tend to set our teeth on edge. I'm talking about our growing through little things daily.

Let me illustrate by using a part of a letter from a friend of mine. He writes,

> The other night I got a call from a brother in our church whose plumbing had just burst in the ceiling of his two-year-old home, ruining ceilings in three rooms along with carpet, padding, and walls in those areas. Damage soared into the hundreds of dollars.
>
> After the cleanup operations were complete I said to him, "Buddy, how are you holding up under all this? Are you still on top of it with the Lord?"
>
> His reply was a classic: "Yeah, I can handle the big things with the Lord. For some reason they're the easy ones to give thanks for. My problem is some of the little things which happen which bug me to death. Often those are the tough things to let go."

The same is often true with me. I got cheated out of thousands of bucks on a crooked "Christian" land deal and was able to turn it over to the Lord instantly. But, on the other hand, I'll go through the supermarket line and get ripped off for 29 cents when the gal fails to honor a coupon, and when I get home and realize the mistake I sometimes find myself sulking for an hour or two.

My friend's true-to-life exposé is so typical and so normal that it is almost humorous. How often have we seen the same thing happen in our own homes?

I remember before Dick and I were born-again people, our ten-month-old daughter, Laurie, had a sinus infection that put her on the hospital's critical list for more than two weeks. It was interesting that even though our marriage was already splitting and we rarely prayed separately, much less together, there we stood outside Laurie's intensive care ward clinging to each other tightly and praying fervently with all our mights. The minute the crisis was over, however, we went back to fighting the cold war of emotional divorce.

Several years later after we had accepted Christ, we saw the emergence of a familiar pattern. Given a big crisis, we rushed, no, raced wildly into God's presence, sought His face, quoted Scripture, and almost immediately found His peace and lost our panic. However, if we had to face a daily trauma—a short, snide remark spoken by a Christian brother or sister or a bank teller asking for **more** identification before cashing our check—we went to pieces.

The key is in the words "we went." In one case we

instantly went to the Lord; in the other, we went slowly and after much pessimistic brooding. What we lost by late action, besides valuable time, was the ability to cope. It never seems to occur to us in daily trivia to go immediately to the Lord with our attitudes and festering spirits.

For years I have been able to withstand the enormous pressures of traveling, but a number of years ago I regularly and habitually fell apart whenever the airlines lost my luggage.

Then once, when I landed in Atlanta—and my luggage went on to Puerto Rico—I was just about to dive into the pool of panic when, very quietly, I heard from within . . . "Why don't you run to Me and trust Me to do My work in you?"

I wondered what work the Lord could possibly do in me when my luggage, which was off vacationing in San Juan, held my clothes, my notes, and my well-marked Bible. But as it dawned on me that the Lord knew about this before it happened, I accepted the fact that He must have other plans. Calmly, I told the airline official where I would be speaking for the next three days and asked him to send my wayward suitcases over when they returned.

As it turned out, speaking in my slightly more than grubby pants suit and using no notes won the hearts of my non-Christian audience, and we saw God use the luggage loss, a most vexing daily problem, to His glory. To this day, each time an airline loses by luggage, a small song starts inside of me. It's rather interesting to anticipate what new thing God is about to work.

I have to admit I wish I were this quick to run to Him on **all** daily vexations, but I **am** learning. The secret is to go immediately to the Lord. He wants us to be faithful in little things and to realize His sovereignty in all things. Evidently He wants to help us handle the dailies as well as the heavies, if we will turn to Him first.

We can grow through **differences** and through **daily** events and circumstances, and finally, believe it or not, we can grow through **doubt.**

Not long ago I watched a television documentary about Germany's Adolph Hitler. The film dealt with his early conquests. After he was shown as conquerer of the last country in a series of takeovers, the narrator said, "Now, with this latest triumph, Hitler took away the German people's freedom to doubt."

I was and still am fascinated with the phrase "freedom to doubt" because we usually do not associate freedom with doubt. It is safer by far to impose a "no freedom to doubt" rule; and Hitler, realizing this and not willing to risk the consequences, made sure that any doubt of his "right" to rule was not expressed openly. He removed the peoples' freedom to doubt.

Robert Browning once wrote,

> Who knows most,
> Doubts most.

In some circles it is a sin to doubt; yet often our

133

times of doubt lead us on a search for truth, and once more the growing process is enhanced.

Several years ago one of our friends joined a religious cult. He jumped in with both feet and began an almost hysterical witnessing campaign to convert his friends. Dick and I knew we were on his list and sure enough one day, for four hours, he ranted and raved, produced seventeen Scriptures to every one of ours, and raised more doubts in our hearts than Carter has little liver pills.

"You are not believers," he shouted, pleaded, begged, and repeated. Dick's reaction was very German. He just got quiet and grew taller. My typical Irish-Hungarian temperament did its usual thing: flared, angered, simmered, and exploded in an endless cycle.

I will never forget our ride home after that ghastly afternoon. Our emotions ran from anger right straight to doubt. Our friend had used Scripture and had won every logical argument, and Dick and I were as defeated as any football team who has lost every game for three years straight. But a funny thing happened on our way to linking up with defeat.

When we got home we made a beeline for our Bibles to see exactly what we believed and why. Our doubt became the greatest motivation for spiritual growth that we had ever had.

Those terrible doubts forced us to search out the Word of God in a way neither of us ever could have guessed. For days, we read, prayed, and conversed about our faith, and when we emerged from the long

134

tunnel of doubt, we knew once and for all where we stood as believers, why we believed as we did, what our theological positions were, and who we were when we called ourselves "children of God."

Our friend still tries to convert us from time to time, and he still thinks we are lost, but I love him because he made us doubt. He made us doubt the reality of Jesus as God, he cast doubts on our Christian daily life-style, and most assuredly he made the dubious prediction about our chances for eternal life. In short, he forced us to doubt our whole Christian experience, and God used that afternoon and several since to help us become even stronger in the Lord.

I am not blind to the destructive nature of doubt nor to how wrong it is to maintain a continually doubting spirit, but I do believe that God sometimes uses doubt to strengthen our faith.

I love the doubting disciple Thomas. I suspect that the reason he was allowed to see Jesus in person was precisely because he had so thoroughly doubted the other disciples' testimony regarding the Resurrection. I'm sure his faith was stronger and more durable after his personal encounter with the risen Christ.

I love, too, the attitude of the disciples toward Thomas's negative and doubting spirit. They didn't get angry with him; they didn't shut him off or ostracize him from their group of believing, excited hearts. They simply said, "Thomas, wait until you see Jesus for yourself." They knew Thomas's doubts would not be answered by human explanations, but by the Man Himself.

Sometimes God uses a person, an illness, an accident, the loss of a loved one, or the loss of a job to shake up the troops; but often the doubts such circumstances produce lead us to great harvests of growth.

These three "d's"—**differences, daily,** and **doubt**—can be stumbling blocks that trip us up every time we take a step. Or, they can be part of God's lovely path leading toward real growth. If we take that path we grow into the man or woman of God He wants us to be.

Chapter Seven

Growing Through Continuing

> I would not give much for your religion
>   unless it can be seen.
> Lamps do not talk,
> But they **do** shine.
>   —Charles Haddon Spurgeon

Most of us, myself included, want to talk, write, or inform others of our faith. Very few of us want to be quiet, shining lamps, reflecting God's glory as Spurgeon has described.

Yet the growing process, as I have observed it for the past twenty years, is not always accomplished by great thrusts of movements, electrifying words or verbal exchanges, highly publicized preaching and gimmicks, or prolonged bursts of frenzied activity. More often than not—in fact, you could say it's the rule

rather than the exception—Christian growing takes place during the
> still quiet times of waiting
> and our years of
> simply continuing to continue.

My mother often remarked about the great many times God would seem to give the frustrating answer of "wait" to our prayers instead of a clearly defined, decisive yes or no. She was fascinated by the blocks of time a child of God spends in God's waiting room. In one place in her diary she wrote,

> Christians today, as always, are waiting on God to answer their prayers. Many have waited long and have doubted God has heard. Others have become offended, especially when God has said "No," or worse yet, "Not now," and have charged God foolishly. When Job's whole life went out the window the Scripture says, "In all of this Job did not sin or charge God with wrong" (Job 1:22, RSV).
>
> God's waiting room is the most tiresome and unpleasant place in our Christian experience. We do not like delays or denials, for hasn't God said, "Ask, and it shall be given you"? (Matt. 7:7). God has reasons for delays. Some He will reveal to us, others we may never know, but one thing we know for certain—God never makes a mistake!

Most of us know all about waiting rooms.

• If we are waiting in a doctor's office, we sit all glassy-eyed, idly thumbing through one magazine after another.

• If we are waiting in a restaurant for a table, we

periodically hassle the hostess into showing us her list to prove she hasn't forgotten us.

• If we are waiting in our car trying to start it and the battery is dead, or the crossing light is stuck on red, our fingers drum out impatient tunes on our steering wheel. And the verbal language we use is not exactly lyrics for a musical.

• If we are left waiting in some hospital room or corridor for tests, X rays, or surgery, our spirits angrily question not only the whys, the financial cost of it all, but for the life of us we can't figure out this most inopportune delay.

• If you have ever waited on the Lord for a decision involving

deciding on a mate,
finding a job,
changing a career or vocation,
buying a house or car,
getting pregnant,
adopting a child,
recovering from major surgery or a coronary,
coping with a prodigal son or daughter,
working for disagreeable or unqualified people, or
adjusting to unfair or unjust situations,

then you can count yourself a member of a very large group.

In short, we are activists. We are not given to large amounts of tolerability when it comes to waiting or continuing. In our veritable storm of noisy activities and frantic desires to achieve success, we come to loathe the waiting-room experiences of life.

I'm Still Growing

We stand up in church, discard our hymnal, and sing steadily and from memory,

> Have thine own way, Lord!
> Have thine own way.
> Thou art the potter,
> I am the clay.
>
> Mould me and make me after thy will,
> While I am waiting,
> Yielded and still.*

But as soon as church is over, we rush back out into our tense, stress-filled world, and we neither wait nor become yielded or still.

Our song, sung so valiantly in church, turns out to be nothing more than a flag of hypocrisy—gross, unattractive, and merely a flapping banner in the wind.

Why do we hate the waiting and the continuing experience so much? Why do we long to do anything but wait? What is it in our nature that drives us to productivity, speed, and impatience like a tennis ball volleying back and forth across the nets of life? Why is waiting or continuing so difficult a task? And why do we think that to be quiet or still at times shows some kind of lack of intelligence?

I do not have the answers to these questions. However, I have had a lot of practice at waiting, and I can tell you this: I don't like waiting any more than you do. But I have learned and am satisfied knowing that the

*G. C. Stebbins, "Have Thine Own Way, Lord" (Carol Stream, Ill.: Hope Publishing Co., 1935). (Original copyright 1907; renewed in 1935 by G.C. Stebbins.) Used by special permission.

Lord uses our waiting-room experiences to bring about a new dimension in our growing.

Here are some observations about waiting and continuing that may help during your times of coping.

1. **Waiting out a time in God's waiting room never comes easily or automatically to any of us.**

Our attitude toward it will determine our demise or our development.

2. **The waiting process is used by God to force, slam, or shove us into a position of trust and dependence on Him.**

It is vital to our Christian experience to continually set our hearts on God in obedient trust and dependence. I wish we could all magically obey the Lord, do His will, and fall dutifully in line like good soldiers. But most of us, given that free will of ours, have to be forced into the waiting room before we give God our undivided attention! And sometimes we find we are not only to wait on the Lord, but also we're to take a back row seat, completely removed from the action!

Dick and I have become grandparents. Nine months ago our son and daughter-in-law presented us with a beautiful little granddaughter named April Joy.

No matter where I am or how busy my schedule is, I write April a letter each month. (Of course, April can't read, but her mother is saving the letters.)

About two months ago, little April had been visiting us on a Friday. Late that afternoon, her parents came to take her home. As she sat in her car seat, April helped me crystalize some thoughts on waiting, continuing, and taking a back seat.

On Sunday of that weekend, Dick and I left for San Francisco and I wrote April her monthly letter. I didn't intend to include my personal letter to her in a book, but because there is such confusion and anxiety about waiting, I thought it might help you clarify your thinking on this subject.

Hi, darling girl,

The last I saw of you Friday, you were sitting all strapped and buckled in your car seat in the back of your parents' little red Volkswagon. You were not crying, fussing, or fidgeting, but you were definitely less than thrilled. You sat back there, your tiny mouth all set in a tight, grim little line, sober as a judge, and clearly you communicated,

1. I don't want to leave Grandma's house and go home.
2. I don't care for sitting back here while my parents ride up front and have all the fun!

You made my heart smile, darling girl, because I saw so much of me in you. I couldn't cajole you into a good-bye smile or wave at all, but I loved you so much in that moment because you pointed out a truth I needed to define a bit better.

You see, the noble truth is that much of life we sit in the back seat somewhere, buckled into our chair alone and forced to wait it out. We are not sure what we are waiting for, but somehow we are forced into that undeniable corner of trusting—because we have no other place to turn to!

142

So, trust you did! Not gleefully or with your usual joyous squealing, but respectfully, somberly, and with a will to continue. How dear you looked as you waited out your back-seat experience.

Believe it or not, your parents had your welfare clearly in mind, and even as you sat back there, not too sure of your parents' motives, they were taking excellent and loving care of you.

The seat straps and buckles were all for your protection and safety. That car seat was not designed to imprison or restrict you, but to **preserve** you.

Your parents drove you home because there they can best properly feed, bathe, and bed you down in your own sweet little white crib.

I see a perfect picture in this in regard to our relationship to God and His care of us. And I wonder why it is, when we think some cruel act of fate has us sitting all alone in the back seat or in some waiting room, that we are so hesitant to look forward? So reluctant to look in the seat ahead of us or to the side and see that God is definitely in the driver's seat and taking good care of us?

Darling girl, God was particularly watching over your precious family that very afternoon because while you sat back there waiting, unhappy, and full of unanswered questions, the Lord pointed out a small, charming house to a real estate lady and the next day the wheels were set in motion for your parents to have their very own first house. I know you don't know anything about California real estate but, baby, it's an outrageous, impossible problem. Yet God honored your parents' prayers and their waiting, and so your early life and future will be spent in that dear, treasured place.

There, you see? Even as you sat quietly questioning

143

everything in the back seat, God was moving (literally) for your good.

He is a marvelous God, and the first prayer I will teach you to say is, "Jesus, I love you."

Grandpa and I are here in San Francisco for three days. Grandpa is working for the bank and I am (hopefully) writing another book—so I must get to it.

I love you, darling girl. Eat your vegetables as well as the yummies like peaches, pears and crunchy bread sticks!

Lovingly,

Grandma

Perhaps there is no way to come to a full position of trust except through the waiting-room and back-seat experiences.

As I look at the lives of marvelous, shining, lamp-like Christians of our times and biblical times, I see once more that growth, maturity, and spiritual accomplishments are achieved through waiting and continuing.

In a taped sermon called "Growing Through Waiting," my friend Pastor Chuck Swindoll made a survey of the Bible's wait-ers. His list included both the names of and the numbers of years each person mentioned spent buckled into the back seat somewhere:

Noah   —who waited 120 years before it rained,
Job   —who waited perhaps a lifetime, 60-70 years,

Abraham—who waited 100 years to find a city and
         never did,
Joseph   —who served 14 years of imprisonment
         because of false accusations,
Moses   —who waited 40 years in the desert.

I figured those years added up to over three hundred
years of waiting, divided among five men. Then Pastor
Swindoll mentioned in passing other wait-ers such as
these Old Testament men: Samson, Samuel, Gideon,
and the prophets. Rev. Swindoll also talked of New
Testament men, starting with Jesus—who is the
prime example of a wait-er—The Twelve, and Paul.
Then he added this interesting zinger: "Most of the
men who waited never realized their dreams or saw
their hopes materialize."

How true. Perhaps this is exactly what we find the
most difficult about waiting. We are deeply programmed to see the end product, the completion of a
task, and the final outcome. In short, we are **result
seekers, not continuers.** We have to be successful.
We have to bring forth the evidence or we have failed in
our mission. For the Christian that means producing
so many born-again bodies, bringing so many new
people to Sunday school, and adding names to the
church membership roll. We seem to think that adding
numbers is the only way to grow. But the man-made
criteria for success and achievement are not God's
ways.

Perhaps part of our confusion lies in the fact that

there are many time lapses in the Bible. I'm not sure the exact reason for it, but often the Word of God leaves out many years of ordinary, rather monotonous days of living.

Take, for example, Paul's missionary journeys. Those trips probably consumed the better part of **thirty-five** years of his life, yet the Scriptures appear to read as if it all happened within a three-year period. It's no wonder then when we read the account and see the achievements of Paul's "three-year" ministry, that we feel great frustrations because three years of our lives show so little in comparison. We become uptight with our lack of progress or our slow rate of growth because we want to live exciting, spiritual lives, and we feel we are not. We tend to forget that much of life is made up of ordinary, uneventful days. As a woman, I think of waiting days as days filled not with writing books, having dinner with a publisher, speaking to a large audience or taping a television show but with ironing, simmering stew on the back burner of my stove, and finally getting to the buttons and the mending.

We seem to show signs of irritability if our lives are narrowed down to a waiting-room period, a back-seat assignment, or a day intellectually limited by mundane chores. Yet, who among us could stand the strain of an exciting, miracle-a-minute existence?

Our Father who made us knew long before we arrived here that we would need the quiet, ordinary, even boring days to sit back, to put our confidence and trust in Him, and to learn about God's leading.

146

Evangelist Joe Arnett once said, "To learn God's will, take your gifts, buckle down, and use your talents in the local church as if you plan to stay there all your life. God will move you if He wants."

Over and over the psalmist talks of being still and waiting on the Lord. We must begin to see the times of waiting for what they really are: long-term growth.

Then too, there's the problem of our timing and God's timing. Unfortunately, God's timing never seems to line up with ours. We seem to beg Him for various things and we tell Him these are **needs,** not wants, and still **His** timing dictates the answers. I'm not sure why I have to relearn this concept about God's timing so many times a year, but I do.

Here is an interesting perspective put on our prayers and God's lesson in timing by my friend Ruth Calkin.

THANK YOU FOR WAITING

> Had you given in to me, Lord
> On the thing I wanted so much,
> My life today
> Would be a sorry mess.
> I tell you nothing new—
> I simply repeat
> What you told me
> Long, long ago.
> Finally today I see it—
> From your point of view.
> Thank you for not giving in to me.

147

> Thank you most of all
> For patiently waiting
> For me to give in to you.*

The line that touches me the most is "Thank you for not giving in to me—." As I look back on my times of waiting and wanting, I see what a tragedy it would have been for God to have given in and released me from my waiting-room experiences.

Sometime, as a small project, write down some of the things you have begged God for and then count up how many times He didn't deliver your demands. As I read over my list, I could shout for joy because He denied my requests and kept me strapped in a back seat, out of action. Generally hindsight allows us to see the whole picture.

I am unashamedly and admittedly deeply in love with an Old Testament prophet named Habakkuk. He single-handedly has taught me more about using the waiting and continuing times and about trusting God with the "whole picture" concept than any man, dead or alive.

What a delightful, real honest-to-God man Habakkuk must have been. His book, fifth from the end of the Old Testament and only three chapters long, is a study in the frustrations of waiting and continuing without viable results.

Briefly, chapter 1 begins with Habakkuk shouting out about the "whys" of his life. Listen to his mounting frustration as he yells,

*Ruth Harms Calkin, **Tell Me Again, Lord, I Forget** (Elgin, Ill.: David C. Cook Publishing Co., 1974), p. 61. Used by permission.

O Lord, how long must I call for help before you will listen? I shout to you in vain; there is no answer. "Help! Murder!" I cry, but no one comes to save. Must I forever see this sin and sadness all around me?

Wherever I look there is oppression and bribery and men who love to argue and to fight. The law is not enforced and there is no justice given in the courts, for the wicked far outnumber the righteous, and bribes and trickery prevail (Hab. 1:2–4, TLB).

Bless his dear heart. I know just how he felt. He had had it! He was sick of waiting around while all hell broke loose, while no one came to his rescue, and while evil enemies and their deeds prevailed.

The Lord's answer indicates that God was not angry or displeased with Habakkuk's outburst; but God's answer was of a most different vein than Habakkuk had expected. God proceeded to tell the prophet that things were going to get a **whole lot worse** before they got a whole lot better.

Habakkuk was genuinely shocked and I imagine his voice was choked with horror as he sputtered, "O, Lord my God, my Holy One, you who are eternal—is your plan in all of this to wipe us out? Surely not!" (Hab. 1:12, TLB).

And Habakkuk ends the first chapter with two burning questions to the Lord: "Will you let them get away with this forever? Will they succeed forever in their heartless wars?" (Hab. 1:17, TLB).

Clearly Habakkuk was as frustrated as you and I about life on this planet; yet somehow, someway he shook the cobwebs out of his mind and figured there were no options left, no courses of action open, and no alternatives available but **to wait on God.**

I can see him now, tugging on his full white beard and beginning the second chapter with his declaration, "I will climb my watchtower now, and **wait to see** what answer God will give to my complaint" (Hab. 2:1, TLB, emphasis mine).

Then gently Habakkuk records the voice of God saying,

> "Write my answer on a billboard, large and clear, so that anyone can read it at a glance and rush to tell the others. But these things I plan won't happen right away. Slowly, steadily, surely, the time approaches when the vision will be fulfilled. If it seems slow, do not despair, for these things will surely come to pass. Just be patient! They will not be overdue a single day!
>
> "Note this: Wicked men trust themselves alone [as these Chaldeans do], and fail; but the righteous man trusts in me, and lives!" (Hab. 2:2-4, TLB).

We have no way of knowing how long Habakkuk was silent before the Lord or how many days he waited there, for we have one of those time lapses again; but we do know God waited with him.

Habakkuk's lessons have taught me that:

• We have to wait in silence. Times of waiting are not the times to run here and there telling people our terrible tales of woe. These are not times to converge with close friends and engage in a pity party. Instead we are to be **still** and **know** that God is God, sovereign and sufficient for our ability to continue.

150

- We have to learn to blindly trust God **before** we see results or successful conclusions.
- We have to understand that no matter how dark the picture becomes, God will still be in control and will still be the **only** light of the world.

I am glad that darling Habakkuk did not end his book saying that everything had been worked out, that his enemies had been defeated, or that he was full of the right answers. On the contrary, while Habakkuk's last chapter is a song to be sung with soloists, choirs, and stringed instruments, he ends his book with these lyrics, "I will quietly wait for the day of trouble to come upon the people who invade us" (Hab. 3:16, TLB).

He writes his song not seeing results, not having achievements to present, and not experiencing a visible success. Yet he ends with,

> Even though the fig trees are all destroyed, and there is neither blossom left nor fruit, and though the olive crops all fail, and the fields lie barren; even if the flocks die in the fields and the cattle barns are empty, yet I will rejoice in the Lord; I will be happy in the God of my salvation. The Lord God is my Strength, and he will give me the speed of a deer and bring me safely over the mountains (Hab. 3:17–19, TLB).

He has decided to continue to continue. What a lesson! What a prophet! What a God! And the best news of all is that Habakkuk's God is still the same today.

For more than ten years now I have traveled extensively for the chaplains' division of the United States

Army. I have spoken for large and small audiences of soldiers and their families, for military personnel in remote (even classified) bases, for the wives of military men in almost every state of the union, and I have taken four exhausting trips overseas. However, the military work—speaking and singing—that demanded the most from me in terms of energy, effectiveness, and real healing came from the speaking tours to the wards in military hospitals.

I have seen more waiting and continuing done in those hospitals than any place on the face of the earth.

In 1970, before the Vietnam conflict was drawn to a conclusion, I spoke in Japan at Camp Zama. I did many engagements there for military personnel, including women's luncheons, couples' banquets, high school assemblies, and seven wards of Camp Zama's hospital.

I set up a ward program with the chaplains that allowed me to sing four or five numbers in each ward. Then I would give a brief ten-minute testimony, and finally I was able to spend a few minutes bedside with as many boys as there was time for.

On the elevator in Zama's hospital, as we neared the floor where I was to do my very first military hospital performance, the Red Cross worker who accompanied the chaplains and me said rather casually, "The patients you'll be singing and speaking for are all in our open-wound wards, but we feel they need you the most." I nodded, feeling I could handle it. Little did I know.

I had not heard the term "open-wound ward" before,

and even though I suspected what it meant I was in no way prepared for it. When we pushed through the first doors I saw before me men and boys fresh off the battlefield. Some had been air-lifted in only hours before and were still covered with Vietnam mud. Their bloody wounds were all uncovered, and the air was thick with the angry hopelessness of waiting.

Never had I felt so unequal to a task. My first thoughts were a sheer mess of panic-stricken, mumbled phrases.

But escaping was impossible, and so I smiled and stumbled over to the piano. The nurses pushed the ambulatory patients close beside me—and somehow, by the loving work of God, I swallowed the knot in my throat, tried to ignore the boy with half of his face covered with a bloody mass of pus, and sang my well-rehearsed numbers.

They were a marvelous, attentive, appreciative audience, and like all great audiences they began to pull the very best of everything from me.

I can never remember a time of singing any better, speaking and relating more directly to hurting hearts, or having a faster sense of humor. It was as if all my previous speaking and singing performances were merely a warm-up rehearsal for this one. This was the real thing, and God didn't waste one single experience or song or conversation between the soldiers and me.

That first day I laughed and cried with those men and sang and spoke in seven open-wound wards before noon.

It was in the last ward that morning, just before we

153

left the hospital, that I felt compelled to turn and talk to just one more boy. I asked if there was time, and the chaplain glanced at his watch and okayed five more minutes.

In the first bed I saw, as I turned back to the ward, a young black soldier lay somberly looking at me. As I took the two or three steps to his side, I noticed he had no visible wounds or scars, and the blankets were neatly up around his chest.

I kidded him about his taking up a bed in this ward, when obviously there was nothing wrong with him. We teased back and forth for a minute and then I said, "Hey, no kidding, how come you're here? You look so well and I see no wounds."

He had been smiling, but he lost it and said quite simply, "Well, ma'am, the surgeons are upstairs right now, and they are deciding on whether or not they will amputate my legs. I'm just lyin' here waiting for their decision."

His words took my breath away, and I felt as if someone had swung a baseball bat directly to my middle.

"Is that scary?" was all I could manage.

"Yes, ma'am, it is," he answered.

I've never been in danger of losing an arm or leg or anything—except the end of my little finger once while I was slicing a Christmas ham—and so I was at a loss to relate to him. But I asked, "How do you feel about it?"

"I guess I'm mad and a little bitter, ma'am," he said. "I've got a baby son whom I've never seen before and I

154

don't want to go home half a man. If they take my legs off, they are going to do it here," he said, pointing to his thighs. "I don't want my kid to see no half a man. I want to be a whole man or I don't want to go home."

His face lost its pleasantness, and the anger of his words and feelings wrote themselves into his expression.

I honestly did not know how to respond to him, and to my surprise I found myself asking, "May I pray about this?"

Instantly, he said, "Oh, yes," and closed his eyes.

I felt idiotic, for there I stood, not having the slightest glimmer of insight on **how to pray.** I thought, **I'm no Billy Graham. What am I doing here?**

And then, because the Lord is our ever-present help in trouble, I remembered a part of a sermon our pastor preached before I left California. He said a psychiatrist in San Francisco had declared that man's greatest problem was his brokenness and that his greatest need was to be made whole.

So I began to pray. I don't remember the exact words, but I do remember most of the content. In general, here's how it went:

Oh, Lord, all morning I have seen broken men waiting for some kind of miracle. I've seen men without faces, arms, legs or parts of chests, stomachs or backs, and it has been horrible.

But worse than that, and sadder still, are the men who wait here with fragmented hearts, and shattered souls; hearts that have never known the forgiveness of God or

155

never held the healing peace of God, and who never have experienced the wholeness of their manhood.

So, Lord, I don't know how to pray for the doctors upstairs, but I do know that You are the only one who can really make this man whole. You are the only forgiver of sins, the healer of wounds and giver of life; so touch this man, with or without his legs, and make him whole.

The soldier startled me by shouting not "Amen," but whooping out, "WOW! That's what I needed!"

Then he lifted up his head from the pillow and called loudly for the chaplains. It seemed to me that fifteen chaplains responded immediately, for we were instantly surrounded.

"Tell them upstairs, go up and tell them," he said excitedly, "that I can take their decision now. Whatever they decide, I can take it. I've been worrying about the wrong thing! I'm whole in here," he thumped his chest, "and that's what counts. So you go tell 'em—I'm ready."

It was the seventh time that morning my mascara and makeup were ruined. I stumbled out those doors, weeping and stunned with the way God operates.

One year later I returned to Japan and Camp Zama. When I got to the hospital I said to the first chaplain I met, "Say, do you remember a black soldier who was . . . ." and the chaplain's face lit up like a Christmas tree.

"I've been waiting to tell you about him, Mrs. Landorf."

Then the chaplain told me that the doctors' verdict

that day was not to amputate but to do surgery in a last ditch effort to save the soldier's legs. The surgery was a complete success, and six weeks later the soldier was sent home.

"But let me tell you about his last six weeks of convalescing here, Mrs. Landorf," the chaplain continued. "It was incredible! Even though he was in a wheelchair, he went to every ward in the hospital and told anyone who would listen, and a few who wouldn't, about the day he became 'whole.' He wrote his wife and family telling them of his conversion. He was almost hysterical with joy when he read a letter to me about his wife's attendance at a little church and her acceptance of Christ. Mrs. Landorf, that soldier was the greatest thing that ever happened to this hospital, and none of us will ever forget him."

I have thought of that black soldier so many times. How he struggled with the waiting time, and yet God used both the wounds and the recovery period to make a whole man. What mysterious ways God devises and arranges for all of us, but how beautiful.

Did you know that God can give you a contentment in your waiting-room experience? Even though, like Habakkuk of old or the soldier of this century, you might not see the final result or hear the thunderous applause of success.

Are you fully aware that you have been born into God's family? You are planted in His garden, and it's exactly where He wants you, and for such a time as this!

Whether it's a waiting room or a harvest field, you

157

may be in the only place that makes you totally accessible to God. Don't be discouraged, dear heart. It's God's place, too.

Paul said to his beloved friends at Philippi,

> And I am sure that God who began the good work within you will keep right on helping you grow in his grace until his task within you is finally finished on that day when Jesus Christ returns (Phil. 1:6, TLB).

There it is, the promise to help us grow, to help us endure, to help us not self-destruct in times of stress; and the promise is good for as long as it takes for Christ to return.

David said it beautifully when he said,

> But the godly shall flourish like palm trees, and grow tall as the cedars of Lebanon. For they are transplanted into the Lord's own garden, and are under his personal care. Even in old age they will still produce fruit and be vital and green. This honors the Lord, and exhibits his faithful care. He is my shelter. There is nothing but goodness in him! (Ps. 92:12–15, TLB).

Oh, Lord, thank you for all these different ways of growing. Help us to learn our lessons well, for when we are obedient to you our joy knows no boundaries, our love sets no limits, and wisdom ever broadens.

But we need you, Lord.

Help us to continue to continue to continue . . . .